# DICTIONARY OF
# DEVELOPMENT ECONOMICS

From the same Publisher:

GLOSSARY OF ECONOMICS
English/American, French, German, Russian

GLOSSARY OF FINANCIAL TERMS
English/American, French, Spanish, German

DICTIONARY OF INTERNATIONAL RELATIONS AND POLITICS
German, English/American, French, Spanish

Complete catalogue is available on request.

# DICTIONARY OF
# DEVELOPMENT ECONOMICS

*Economic Terminology*
*In Three Languages*
*English · French · German*

COMPILED AND ARRANGED BY

TRAUTE SCHARF
Associate Industrial Development Officer,
Industrial Policies and Programming Division,
United Nations Industrial Development Organization,
Vienna, Austria

with the cooperation of
MARC BALIN

ELSEVIER PUBLISHING COMPANY
Amsterdam / London / New York
1969

ELSEVIER PUBLISHING COMPANY
335 Jan van Galenstraat
P.O. Box 211, Amsterdam, The Netherlands


ELSEVIER PUBLISHING CO. LTD.
Barking, Essex, England


AMERICAN ELSEVIER PUBLISHING COMPANY, INC.
52 Vanderbilt Avenue
New York, New York 10017

Library of Congress Catalog Card Number: 70-97801

SBN 444-40799-5

Printed in The Netherlands

# INTRODUCTION

The problems of development in the "Third World" are particularly complex. The techniques developed to date to solve these problems appear either inefficient or inadequate. The basic problems of the economic "take-off" and "self-sustained growth" remain unsolved. These are neither automatic processes nor the result of a combination of economic factors, formulated in perfect mathematical models, but with less apparent results.

The terminology[1] of policies of growth and strategies of development - less classic than those of traditional economic analysis - reflects the evolution of techniques and methods of approach. A terminology can offer, however, a useful instrument in the study of these problems and in the search for appropriate solutions.

This justifies the glossary whose principal target is the systematization of the terminology of development, growth and planning at all stages with all their implications in a socio-economic framework. It is difficult to disassociate, in effect, the framework of economic activities from the development process, which explains the flexibility of the contents of this glossary.

Following recent works in lexicology, this glossary has been arranged by subject matter rather than alphabetically. The division in twelve chapters[2] is formal, especially because the socio-economic development process needs an inter-disciplinary approach.

This classification was made for the sake of convenience in order to group together terms which are associated in usage or meaning. Most of the terms relate in some manner to the concepts of more than one chapter. It was attempted to include in this glossary the basic concepts in the field of socio-economic development and those common terms which are distinctive to this field. In this context it seemed more advantageous to take into account the particularities and interdependence among sectors: agriculture and industry on the one hand, and international economic relations and foreign aid on the other.

Besides the normal relations between factors of production, the "tertiary sector"- to use the terminology of Colin Clark - is necessarily divided among the chapters "Manpower", "Industry" and "Transportation and Communication". There are no fixed categories in an evolving science which results from an association of numerous factors.

A special place is reserved for strategies such as planning and for targets such as development which occupy important places in the thinking of countries of the "Third World". These countries, however, after having

---

[1] cf. Traute SCHARF, Entwicklungsländer - Entwicklungshilfe. Glossary: German, English, French. In: Langenscheidt's Lebende Sprachen, No. 2, 1966.

[2] The separate references are numbered consecutively, making them easily discernible. These numbers are repeated in alphabetical indexes in three languages. Thus, the terminology will constitute not only a systematic glossary but also a dictionary.

vi

overcome the stage of "planning fetishism", are searching for more efficient formulas in view of the limited results obtained until now from such planning.

Foreign trade and international economic relations are decisive for young countries. Not only because of the importance of foreign trade, not only because they are "export economies", but because the progressive deterioration in the terms of trade have created unbalanced economic units which in the long term will not be viable and indeed will be incapable of finding in their present structures the means of financing their own development.

The deterioration in the terms of trade highlights the gap between super-industrialized and agricultural societies and the internal contradiction between subsistence economies and export economies, socio-economic organizations which are "more bad than good" integrated in the poorly adapted structures.

The numbering of the different chapters reflects the scientific character of economics and the chapter "Development Statistics" unites the terms of all instruments which foster planning. The statistical services in Africa are still rudimentary; often there is "planning without facts"[3] But the general mathematization of social sciences creates the need to integrate the most recent statistical and mathematical expressions related to planning in the terminology for developing countries.

Finally, the social aspect: education, health and culture seem to be, with sociology, keys to progress. Development is also a social process where archaic structures clash with tools of the atomic era: acculturation of an "under-industrialized" continent with the values and anti-values of "super-industrialized" and automated societies.

After having recognized "the resistance of the minds" and after having included ethnology and anthropology - with which Balandier associated the adjective "political" - it became only more evident that development should be a national process launched from the internal working of the young countries themselves.

This glossary has also been established to promote in a wider framework the standardization of terminology based on the classification in the German language. It is hoped that this work will be useful to young nations and that international organizations as well as research institutes will help to supplement it.

The glossary was undertaken at the United Nations African Institute for Economic Development and Planning, with the decisive support of the Chief of the Documentation Centre at the Institute, Dr. Marc Balin, Docteur ès sciences économiques of the University of Paris.

The author is indebted to the following persons for their help with the final proof reading: Mme Dorothé and Mr. Alexandre Duci (Ambassade de Belgique/Dakar), Herrn Rainer Kühn (Banque Internationale pour le Commerce et l'Industrie du Sénégal/Commerzbank AG. Hamburg), Mr. Randolph Reed and Mr. Albert Williams (Embassy of the United States/Dakar).

---

[3] Wolfgang STOLPER, Planning Without Facts, Harvard University Press, Cambridge, Mass., 1966.

The secretarial work was done in the Pool of IDEP by Mr. Banumu Jobartheh as well as by Miss Henrike Anders, UNIDO, Vienna.

The author will be glad to receive suggestions for improvements in future editions.

Dakar, May 1968                     TRAUTE SCHARF
UNIDO, Vienna, January 1969          Dr.iur.Dr.rer.pol.

# INTRODUCTION

Les problèmes du développement dans les pays du tiers monde sont d'une singulière complexité. Les techniques mises en oeuvre jusqu'à maintenant pour les résoudre se sont révélées ou insuffisantes ou inadaptées. Elles laissent entières le décollage économique et la croissance continue et auto-entretenue qui ne sont ni des processus automatiques, ni le résultat de combinaisons des facteurs économiques dans des modèles à la perfection mathématique certaine, mais aux résultats moins apparents.

La terminologie[1] des politiques de croissance et des stratégies de développement - moins classique que celle de l'analyse économique traditionnelle - reflète l'évolution des techniques et des méthodes d'approche. Elle peut constituer cependant un instrument utile dans l'étude de ces problèmes et la recherche des solutions appropriées.

C'est ce qui justifie ce glossaire dont la finalité est de systématiser le vocabulaire du développement, de la croissance et de la planification à différents niveaux, dans toutes leurs implications et dans leur cadre socio-économique.

Il est difficile de dissocier, en effet le cadre de l'activité économique du processus du développement, ce qui explique la souplesse du plan suivi.

Suivant la tendance moderne en lexicographie, le glossaire "Economie du Développement" est basé sur le classement systématique et non purement alphabétique.

La division en douze chapitres[2] est formelle d'autant que le processus du développement socio-économique demande une approche interdisciplinaire. Cette classification a été introduite afin de grouper les termes qu'il est d'usage d'associer ou dont les sens sont voisins. La plupart des termes se rattachent par certaines côtés où par certaines implications à des notions qui figurent dans plus d'un chapitre.

Le glossaire comprend à la fois des mots clés et des termes d'utilisation courante. Il est dans ce cas plus aisé de tenir compte des particularités et des interactions entre secteurs: agriculture, industrie par. ex., relations économiques internationales d'une côté et aide extérieure d'autre part. Outre les relations normales entre facteurs de production, un secteur - pour reprendre la terminologie chère à Colin Clark - comme "le tertiaire" se retrouve nécessairement dans des chapitres différents, "Main-d'oeuvre", "Industrie", "Transports et Communication" par exemple.

Il n'y a donc pas de catégories figées dans une science en évolution et qui resulte de l'association de nombreux facteurs.

---

[1]  voir Traute SCHARF, Entwicklungsländer - Entwicklungshilfe. Glossaire: allemand, anglais, français. In: Langenscheidt's Lebende Sprachen, No. 2, 1966.

[2]  Chaque expression est numérotée, ce qui facilite le maniement. Ces numéros se retrouveront ensuite dans l'index allemand, anglais et français. Cet index alphabétique pour chacune des trois langues fera de cette terminologie systématique un dictionnaire technique complet.

Une place spéciale est faite à des stratégies comme la planification et à des finalités comme le développement qui occupent une place primordiale dans les préoccupations des pays du tiers monde. Cependant ces pays, après avoir cédé au "Fetichisme du plan" cherchent des formules plus efficaces devant les résultats très humbles obtenus jusqu'ici.

L'importance du commerce extérieur et des relations économiques internationales est également déterminante pour les pays jeunes; non seulement à cause de l'importance du secteur extérieur dans leurs économies, non seulement parce qu'ils sont des "export economies", mais parce que la détérioration progressive des termes de l'échange en a fait des ensembles non homogènes et à long terme incapables de survivre, voire de trouver dans les structures actuelles les moyens du financement de leur développement.

La détérioration des termes de l'échange fait davantage ressortir le décalage entre sociétés super-industrialisées et sociétés agraires et les contradictions internes entre économie de subsistance et culture d'exportation, organisation économique intégrée "tant bien que mal" dans les structures inadaptées.

L'énumération des différents chapitres reflètent des préoccupations qui tiennent compte du caractère scientifique de l'économie, puisque le chapitre "Statistique du Développement" tient à mettre en relief tous les outils nécessaires à la planification. Les services statistiques en Afrique sont encore rudimentaires, on planifie souvent sans données statistiques[3]. Mais la mathématisation générale des sciences sociales abouti à intégrer des expressions relatives des méthodes statistiques et mathématiques les plus récentes pour le développement du tiers monde.

Enfin l'aspect social: éducation, santé, culture, s'est révélé une clé du développement, avec la sociologie bien sûr. Car le développement est aussi un processus social qui confronte des structures archaïques avec les outils de l'ère atomique: "l'acculturation" d'un continent sous-industrialisé avec des valeurs et anti-valeurs d'une civilisation super-industrialisée et automatisée. Depuis que l'on a découvert "la résistance des mentalités", l'ethnologie et anthropologie, qui, associé opportunement par Balandier au mot politique, révèle que le développement est un processus national qui doit être déclencher de l'intérieur des jeunes nations.

La finalité de ce glossaire est de systématiser la terminologie relative au développement et à la planification en introduisant le classement allemand. Notre voeu est qu'il serve aux pays jeunes et que les Organisations Internationales et les Instituts de Recherche nous aident à le compléter. Ce travail a été entrepris à l'Institut de Développement Economique et de Planification des Nations Unies avec le concours déterminant du Chef du Centre de Documentation de l'Institut, Dr. Marc Balin, Docteur ès sciences économiques de l'Université de Paris.

Nous remercions pour une dernière revision Mme Dorothé et Mr. Alexandre Duci, (Ambassade de Belgique / Dakar), Herrn Rainer Kühn, (Banque Internationale pour le Commerce et l'Industrie du Sénégal / Commerzbank AG. Hamburg), Mr. Randolph Reed et Mr. Albert Williams (Embassy of the United States / Dakar).

---

[3] Wolfgang STOLPER, Planning Without Facts, Harvard University Press, Cambridge, Mass., 1966.

Nos remerciements vont aussi au pool de l'IDEP à Mr. Banumu Jobartheh et Mlle Henrike Anders, ONUDI, Vienne.

Nous remercions vivement et souhaitons trouver pour l'achever d'autres compétences et d'autres bonnes volontées.

Dakar, Mai 1968                                TRAUTE SCHARF
ONUDI, Vienne, Janvier 1969          Dr.iur.Dr.rer.pol.

# EINFÜHRUNG

Die Entwicklungsprobleme in den Ländern der "Dritten Welt" sind vielfältig und komplex. Selbst moderne Techniken haben sich oft als unzureichend erwiesen und lassen Probleme wie "Take-Off" und autonomes Wachstum ungelöst. Prozesse, die weder automatisch erfolgen, noch das Resultat einer Kombination von ökonomischen Faktoren sind. Sie werden wohl in perfekten mathematischen Modellen, mit jedoch weniger hervorragenden Ergebnissen dargestellt.

Die Terminologie[1] der Wachstumspolitik und der Entwicklungsstrategie - weniger klassisch als die traditionelle Wirtschaftsanalyse - zeigt die Evolution der Techniken und die Approximationsmethoden auf. Das Vokabular könnte jedoch ein nützliches Instrument in der Untersuchung dieser Probleme und in der Forschung nach adäquaten Lösungen sein.

Dies rechtfertigt das Glossarium, dessen Hauptzweck darin besteht, das Vokabular der Entwicklung, des Wachstums und der Planung zu systematisieren; und zwar auf den verschiedensten Ebenen und in all seinen sozio-ökonomischen Bedeutungen.

Es scheint in der Tat schwierig, die Terminologie des Rahmens der Wirtschaftstätigkeit und des Entwicklungsprozesses zu trennen, woraus sich eine gewisse Elastizität der Gliederung ergibt.

Das Glossarium "Entwicklungsökonomie" ist, den neueren Tendenzen in der Lexikographie folgend, nicht alphabetisch, sondern systematisch angeordnet. Die Klassifikation in zwölf Kapitel[2] ist rein formell; dies umso mehr, als der Prozess der sozio-ökonomischen Entwicklung ein interdisziplinäres Konzept erfordert.

Diese Gruppierung wurde angenommen, um Ausdrücke zusammenzufassen, die man zu assoziieren pflegt und deren Bedeutung ähnlich ist. Die Mehrzahl der Fachausdrücke lässt sich nicht ausschliesslich einem Kapital zuordnen.

Der Autor hat sich bemüht, in diesem Glossar Konzepte von fundamentaler Bedeutung für die sozio-ökonomische Entwicklung zu vereinen; ebenso wie laufende Ausdrücke, die auf diesem Gebiet eine Spezialbedeutung angenommen haben. Es schien auch vorteilhaft, den Besonderheiten und Zusammenhängen zwischen den Sektoren zu folgen. (Landwirtschaft und Industrie, internationale Wirtschaftsbeziehungen einerseits, Auslandshilfe zum anderen).

Neben den Beziehungen zwischen Produktionsfaktoren findet sich der "tertiäre" Sektor - um auf die Terminologie Colin Clarks zurückzugreifen -

---

[1] vgl. Traute SCHARF, Entwicklungsländer - Entwicklungshilfe. Glossar: deutsch, english, französisch. In: Langenscheidt's Lebende Sprachen, No. 2, 1966.

[2] Die einzelnen Ausdrücke sind fortlaufend numeriert, sodass sich eine leichte Lesbarkeit ergibt. In den Registern werden sich diese Nummern wiederholen. Durch diese alphabetischen Register in drei Sprachen wird dieses Glossar - eine systematische Terminologie - gleichzeitig zu einem Fachwörterbuch.

notwendigerweise in einigen Kapiteln so in "Bevölkerung und Arbeitskraft", "Industrie", "Transport und Kommunikation".

Es besteht keine starre Kategorie für eine evolvierende Wissenschaft, die auf der Assoziation zahlreicher Faktoren basiert. Ein besonderer Platz ist der Planung und Zielsetzung der Entwicklung eingeräumt, die den ersten Rang in der Politik der "Dritten Welt" einnehmen. Diese Länder, nachdem sie sich von einem "Planungsfetichismus" befreit hatten, suchen angesichts der bisher bescheidenen Resultate wirksamere Formeln.

Die Wichtigkeit des Aussenhandels und der internationalen Wirtschaftsbeziehungen ist für die jungen Länder ebenfalls bestimmend. Nicht nur wegen der Bedeutung des Aussenhandels für ihre Wirtschaften, nicht nur weil sie vorwiegend Exportwirtschaften sind, sondern weil die progressive Verschlechterung der Terms of trade inhomogene Einheiten geschaffen hat, die nicht langfristig lebensfähig sein können und auch unfähig sind, in der gegenwärtigen Struktur die Finanzierungsmittel für ihre Entwicklung zu finden.

Die Verschlechterung der Terms of trade lässt noch mehr die Diskrepanz zwischen superindustrialisierten- und Agrargesellschaften hervortreten, sowie die internen Widersprüche zwischen Subsistenzwirtschaften und Exportkulturen, Wirtschaftsorganisationen, die eher schlecht als gut in die mangelhafte Struktur integriert sind.

Die Aufzählung der verschiedenen Kapitel zeigt den wissenschaftlichen Charakter dieser Disziplin, insbesondere das Kapitel "Entwicklungsstatistik" versucht, die wissenschaftlichen Instrumente, die der Planung dienen, aufzuzeigen.

Die statistischen Zentren in Afrika sind erst im Entstehen, oft plant man ohne Daten[3]. Jedoch führt die allgemeine Mathematisierung der Sozialwissenschaften dazu, Ausdrücke und Begriffe der jüngsten statistischen und mathematischen Methoden in ein Glossar der Entwicklungsländer aufzunehmen.

Der soziale Aspekt: Erziehung, Gesundheit, Kultur, erwies sich mit der Soziologie als Schlüssel für den Fortschritt. Denn Entwicklung ist auch ein sozialer Prozess, wo archaische Strukturen mit Werkzeugen des Atomzeitalters zusammentreffen: Akkulturation eines "unter-industrialisierten" Kontinentes mit Werten und Anti-Werten "super-industrialisierter" Zivilisationen. Nachdem man den "Widerstand der Gemüter" erkannt hatte und die Ethnologie einschloss, der Balandier das Adjektiv "politisch" assoziierte, wurde es deutlich, dass Entwicklung ein nationaler Prozess sein sollte, der sich vom Landesinnern her entfalten muss.

Dieses Glossarium wurde auch zusammengestellt, um die Standardisierung der Terminologie für Entwicklungsländer in deutscher Sprache zu fördern. Unser Wunsch ist es, dass diese Terminologie den jungen Nationen nützlich sein möge und dass internationale Organisationen und Forschungsinstitute mit ihren Vorschlägen helfen mögen, das Glossarium zu vervollständigen.

Diese Arbeit wurde im Rahmen des African Institute for Economic Development and Planning der Vereinten Nationen durchgeführt, mit der

---

[3] Wolfgang STOLPER, Planning Without Facts, Harvard University Press, Cambridge, Mass., 1966.

xiii

entscheidenden Unterstützung des Leiters des Dokumentationszentrums des Institutes, Dr. Marc Balin, Docteur ès sciences économiques der Universität Paris.

Für die letzte Durchsicht der Fachausdrücke sind wir Zu Dank verpflichtet Mme Dorothé und Mr. Alexandre Duci (Ambassade de Belgique/Dakar), Herrn Rainer Kühn (Banque Internationale pour le Commerce et l'Industrie du Sénégal/Commerzbank AG. Hamburg), Mr. Randolph Reed und Mr. Albert N. Williams (Embassy of the U.S.A./Dakar).

Die Sekretariatsarbeiten wurden im Pool des IDEP von Mr. Banumu Jobartheh, sowie von Frl. Henrike Anders, UNIDO, Wien, durchgeführt.

Für Vorschläge zur Erweiterung und Ergänzung ist der Autor dankbar.

Dakar, Mai 1968
UNIDO, Wien, Jänner 1969

TRAUTE SCHARF
Dr.iur.Dr.rer.pol.

# CONTENTS

# LANGUAGE INDICATION
## LANGUES
## SPRACHEN

| | | | |
|---|---|---|---|
| f | French | français | Französisch |
| d | German | allemand | Deutsch |

# BASIC TABLE

BASIC TABLE

# I.

## DEVELOPMENT
## DEVELOPPEMENT
## ENTWICKLUNG

1 CONCERTED INTER-
NATIONAL ACTION
f Action internationale
concertée
d Gemeinsame, inter-
nationale Aktion

2 DIRECTLY PRODUCTIVE
ACTIVITIES (DPA);
HIRSCHMAN
f Activités directement
productives (ADP)
d Direktproduktive Aktivität

3 ECONOMIC ACTIVITY
f Activité économique
d Wirtschaftliche Aktivität

4 AFRICA SOUTH OF THE
SAHARA
f Afrique au sud du Sahara;
Afrique sud-saharienne
d Afrika südlich der Sahara

5 BLACK AFRICA
f Afrique noire
d Schwarzafrika

6 CENTRAL AFRICA
f Afrique centrale
d Zentralafrika

7 EAST AFRICA
f Afrique de l'est;
Afrique orientale
d Ostafrika

8 ENGLISH-SPEAKING
AFRICA
f Afrique anglophone
d Anglophones Afrika

9 FRENCH-SPEAKING
AFRICA
f Afrique francophone
d Frankophones Afrika

10 INDEPENDENT AFRICA
f Afrique indépendante
d Unabhängiges Afrika

11 NORTH AFRICA
f Afrique du nord
d Nordafrika

12 PRECOLONIAL AFRICA
f Afrique précoloniale
d Präkoloniales Afrika

13 SOUTH AFRICA
f Afrique australe
d Südafrika

14 TROPICAL AFRICA
f Afrique tropicale
d Tropisches Afrika

15 WEST AFRICA
f Afrique de l'ouest
d Westafrika

16 SPLITTING OF AFRICA
f Morcellement de
l'Afrique
d Zersplitterung Afrikas

17 INTER-AFRICAN UNIONS
f Unions interafricaines
d Interafrikanische
Zusammenschlüsse

18 AFRICANISM
f Africanisme;
Etudes africaines
d Afrikanistik

4

41 PUBLIC AID;
   GOVERNMENTAL AID
   f  Aide publique;
      Aide gouvernementale
   d  Staatliche Hilfe

42 TIED AID
   f  Aide conditionnelle
   d  Gebundene Hilfe

43 VOLUME OF AID
   f  Volume de l'aide
   d  Volumen der Hilfe

44 POLICY OF APARTHEID
   f  Politique d'apartheid
   d  Apartheidpolitik

45 EXTERNAL ASSISTANCE
   f  Assistance extérieure
   d  Externe Hilfe

46 MASSIVE ASSISTANCE
   f  Aide massive
   d  "Schockhilfe"

47 MILITARY ASSISTANCE
   f  Assistance militaire
   d  Militärhilfe

48 REQUEST FOR ASSISTANCE
   f  Demande d'assistance
   d  Hilfsgesuch

49 TECHNICAL ASSISTANCE
   f  Assistance technique
   d  Technische Hilfe

50 BILATERALISM
   f  Bilatéralisme
   d  Bilateralismus

51 EASTERN BLOC
   f  Bloc de l'Est
   d  Ostblock

52 ECONOMIC BLOC
   f  Bloc économique
   d  Wirtschaftsblock

53 WESTERN BLOC
   f  Bloc occidental
   d  Westblock

54 BOTTLENECK
   f  Goulot d'étranglement
   d  Engpass

55 CAPACITY TO TRANSFORM;
   KINDLEBERGER
   f  Capacité de trans-
      formation
   d  Transformations-
      fähigkeit;
      Wandlungsfähigkeit

56 ECONOMIC CAPACITY;
   ECONOMIC POWER;
   ECONOMIC RESOURCES
   f  Potentiel économique
   d  Wirtschaftspotential

57 PEACEFUL CO-EXISTENCE
   f  Co-existence pacifique
   d  Friedliche Koexistenz

58 COLONIAL EMANCIPATION
   f  Emancipation des colonies
   d  Koloniale Emanzipation

59 COLONIAL POWERS
   f  Pouvoirs coloniaux
   d  Kolonialmächte

60 COLONIAL STRUCTURE
   f  Structure de l'époque
      coloniale
   d  Kolonialstruktur

61 FORMER COLONIAL
   TERRITORIES
   f  Anciens territoires
      coloniaux
   d  Ehemalige Kolonial-
      gebiete

62 COLONIZATION
   f  Colonisation
   d  Kolonisation

63 COMMUNITY DEVELOPMENT
    f  Développement commu-
       nautaire
    d  Gemeindeentwicklung

64 DARK CONTINENT
    f  Continent noir
    d  Schwarzer Kontinent

65 BENEFICIARY COUNTRY
    f  Pays bénéficiaire
    d  Empfängerland

66 ADVANCED COUNTRY;
    DEVELOPED COUNTRY
    f  Pays nantis;
       Pays avancé;
       Pays développé
    d  Entwickeltes Land

67 DEVELOPING COUNTRY;
    EMERGING COUNTRY
    f  Pays en voie de développe-
       ment;
       Jeunes nations; PERROUX
    d  Entwicklungsland

68 DONOR COUNTRY
    f  Pays donateur
    d  Geberland

69 ECONOMICALLY UNDER-
    DEVELOPED COUNTRY
    f  Pays économiquement
       sous-développé
    d  Wirtschaftlich unterent-
       wickeltes Land

70 INDUSTRIAL COUNTRY
    f  Pays industriel
    d  Industrieland

71 LOW INCOME COUNTRY
    f  Pays à revenu bas;
       Pays à revenu faible
    d  Land mit niedrigem
       Einkommen

72 MAGHREB COUNTRIES
    f  Maghreb
    d  Maghreb-Staaten

73 MOTHER COUNTRY
    f  Métropole
    d  Metropole; Mutterland

74 OIL-RICH COUNTRY
    f  Pays pétrolifère
    d  Öl-Land

75 PARTNER COUNTRY
    f  Pays partenaire
    d  Partnerland

76 RECIPIENT COUNTRY
    f  Pays bénéficiaire
    d  Empfängerland

77 DECOLONIZATION
    f  Décolonisation
    d  Dekolonisation

78 DEMONSTRATION EFFECT;
    DUISENBERRY,
    MYRDAL
    f  Effet de démonstration
    d  Demonstrationseffekt

79 DEPRESSION
    f  Crise
    d  Krise

80 DOMINATION
    f  Domination;
       PERROUX
    d  Domination

81 ECONOMIC DUALISM
    f  Dualisme économique
    d  Wirtschaftlicher
       Dualismus

82 DEVELOPMENT AGENT
    f  Agent du développement
    d  Entwicklungshelfer

83 DEVELOPMENT AGENCY
    f  Organisme officiel de
       développement
    d  Entwicklungsdienst

84  DEVELOPMENT AREA
    f  Zone de développement
    d  Entwicklungsgebiet

85  DEVELOPMENT ASSISTANCE
    f  Assistance au
       développement
    d  Aufbauförderung

86  DEVELOPMENT CHANCES
    f  Chances du développement
    d  Entwicklungschancen

87  DEVELOPMENT COMMIS-
    SIONER;
    DEVELOPMENT OFFICER
    f  Chargé de services de
       développement
    d  Entwicklungsbeamter

88  DEVELOPMENT COMPANY
    f  Société de développement
    d  Entwicklungsgesellschaft

89  DEVELOPMENT DECADE
    f  Décennie de développe-
       ment
    d  Entwicklungsdekade

90  SECOND DEVELOPMENT
    DECADE (DD2)
    f  Deuxième décennie de
       développement
    d  Zweite Entwicklungs-
       dekade (1970-1980)

91  DEVELOPMENT HOMES
    f  Foyers de développement
    d  Entwicklungszellen

92  DEVELOPMENT IDEOLOGY
    f  Idéologie du développe-
       ment
    d  Entwicklungsideologie

93  DEVELOPMENT MEETING
    f  Conférence des pays en
       voie de développement
    d  Entwicklungskonferenz

94  DEVELOPING NATION
    f  Nation en voie de
       développement
    d  Entwicklungsnation

95  DEVELOPMENT NEEDS
    f  Besoins du développement
    d  Entwicklungsbedürfnisse

96  DEVELOPMENT PLANS
    f  Plans de développement
    d  Entwicklungspläne

97  DEVELOPMENT POLITICS
    f  Politique du développement
    d  Entwicklungspolitik

98  DEVELOPMENT
    PROGRAMME
    f  Programme de développe-
       ment
    d  Entwicklungsprogramm

99  DEVELOPMENT PROJECT
    f  Projet du développement
    d  Entwicklungsprojekt

100 DEVELOPMENT STRATEGY
    f  Stratégie du développement
    d  Entwicklungsstrategie

101 DEVELOPMENT TENDEN-
    CIES;
    DEVELOPMENT TRENDS
    f  Tendances de développe-
       ment
    d  Entwicklungstendenzen

102 CAPACITY FOR
    DEVELOPMENT
    f  Capacité de développement
    d  Entwicklungskapazität

103 INTERNATIONAL
    COMPETITION TO ECONO-
    MIC DEVELOPMENT
    f  Compétition internationale
       au développement écono-
       mique
    d  Internationale Entwick-
       lungskonkurrenz

104 LATENESS IN DEVELOP-
MENT
f Retard du développement
d Verspätung in der Ent-
wicklung

105 LEVEL OF DEVELOPMENT
f Niveau de développement
d Entwicklungsniveau

106 MOTIVATION OF
DEVELOPMENT
f Motivation du développement
d Entwicklungsmotivation

107 PATH OF DEVELOPMENT;
TINBERGEN
f Voie de développement
d Entwicklungspfad

108 PROMOTION OF DEVELOP-
MENT
f Promotion du développe-
ment
d Entwicklungsförderung

109 AID FOR DEVELOPMENT
f Aide au développement
d Entwicklungshilfe

110 CASE STUDIES OF
DEVELOPMENT
f Etudes de cas de déve-
loppement
d Fallstudien der Entwicklung

111 NATIONAL CONTROL OF
DEVELOPMENT
f Maîtrise nationale du
développement
d Nationale Kontrolle der
Entwicklung

112 POLE OF DEVELOPMENT
f Pôle de croissance;
PERROUX
d Wachstumspol

113 PROSPECTS OF
DEVELOPMENT
f Perspectives de
développement
d Entwicklungsperspektiven

114 ACCELERATED DEVELOP-
MENT
f Développement accéléré
d Beschleunigte Entwicklung

115 DOCTRINE OF DEVELOP-
MENT
f Doctrine du développement
d Entwicklungsdoktrin

116 ECONOMIC DEVELOPMENT
f Développement économique
d Wirtschaftliche Entwicklung

1-17 OVERALL DEVELOPMENT
f Développement global
d Globale Entwicklung

118 OVERALL DEVELOPMENT
NEEDS
f Exigences du développe-
ment global
d Entwicklungserfordernisse

119 POTENTIAL DEVELOPMENT
f Développement potentiel
d Potentielle Entwicklung

120 SELF-DEVELOPMENT
f Développement autonome
d Autonome Entwicklung

121 SOCIAL DEVELOPMENT
f Développement social
d Soziale Entwicklung

122 RURAL DEVELOPMENT
f Développement rural
d Dorfentwicklung

123 TECHNOLOGICAL
DEVELOPMENT
f Développement technolo-
gique
d Technologische Entwick-
lung

144  ECONOMIC MATURITY
    f  Maturité économique
    d  Wirtschaftliche Reife

145  ECONOMIC OUTLOOK
    f  Perspectives économiques
    d  Wirtschaftsaussichten

146  ECONOMIC PENETRATION
    f  Pénétration économique
    d  Wirtschaftliche Durch-
      dringung

147  ECONOMIC PHILOSOPHY
    f  Philosophie de l'économie
    d  Wirtschaftsphilosophie

148  ECONOMIC POLICY
    f  Politique économique
    d  Wirtschaftspolitik

149  ECONOMIC PROBLEM
    f  Question économique
    d  Wirtschaftsfrage

150  ECONOMIC RECOVERY
    f  Essor économique;
      Redressement économique
    d  Wirtschaftsbelebung

151  ECONOMIC RELATIONS
    f  Rapports économiques
    d  Wirtschaftliche
      Beziehungen

152  ECONOMIC SETTING
    f  Contexte économique
    d  Wirtschaftlicher
      Zusammenhang

153  ECONOMIC SITUATION
    f  Situation économique
    d  Wirtschaftssituation

154  ECONOMIC STABILITY
    f  Stabilité économique
    d  Wirtschaftliche Stabili-
      tät

155  ECONOMIC STUDY
    f  Etude économique
    d  Wirtschaftsstudie

156  ECONOMIC SYSTEM
    f  Système économique
    d  Wirtschaftsform

157  ECONOMIC TRANSITION
    f  Transition économique
    d  Wirtschaftliche Über-
      gangsperiode

158  ECONOMIES OF SCALE
    f  Economies d'échelles;
      Economies dimension-
      nelles
    d  Stückkostendegression

159  COMPETITIVE ECONOMY
    f  Economie compétitive
    d  Konkurrenzfähige
      Wirtschaft

160  CONTINENTAL ECONOMY
    f  Economie continentale
    d  Kontinentale Wirtschaft

161  DOMINATED ECONOMY
    f  Economie dominée;
      PERROUX
    d  Dominierte Wirtschaft

162  DOMINATING ECONOMY
    f  Economie dominante;
      PERROUX
    d  Dominierende Wirtschaft

163  EXPANDING ECONOMY
    f  Economie en voie
      d'expansion
    d  Expandierende Wirtschaft

164  INTERCONTINENTAL
    ECONOMY
    f  Economie intercontinen-
      tale
    d  Interkontinentale Wirt-
      schaft

165  MARKET ECONOMY
    f  Economie de marché;
      Système de libre entre-
      prise
    d  Marktwirtschaft

166 MIXED ECONOMY
    f Economie mixte
    d Soziale Marktwirtschaft

167 ONE-CROP ECONOMY
    f Monoculture
    d Monokultur

168 PLURALISTIC ECONOMY
    f Economie diversifiée
    d Pluralistische Wirtschaft

169 REGIONAL ECONOMY
    f Economie régionale
    d Regionale Wirtschaft

170 SOCIALIST ECONOMY
    f Economie socialiste
    d Sozialistische Wirtschaft

171 SUBSISTENCE ECONOMY
    f Economie de subsistance
    d Subsistenzwirtschaft

172 ECONOMICS OF
    DEVELOPMENT
    f Economie de développe-
      ment
    d Entwicklungswirtschaft

173 AFRICAN ELITE
    f Elite africaine
    d Afrikanische Elite

174 WESTERNIZED ELITE
    f Elite occidentalisée
    d Verwestlichte Elite

175 ENCYCLICA "MATER ET
    MAGISTRA"
    f Encyclique "Mater et
      Magistra"
    d Enzyklika "Mater et
      Magistra";
      JOHANNES XXIII

176 ENCYCLICA "POPULORUM
    PROGRESSIO"
    f Encyclique "Populorum
      progressio"
    d Enzyklika "Populorum
      progressio; PAUL VI

177 ERGONOMICS
    f Ergonomie
    d Ergonomie

178 EURAFRICA
    f Eurafrique
    d Eurafrika

179 EXTRA-AFRICAN
    INTERESTS
    f Intérêts autres qu'afri-
      cains
    d Ausserafrikanische
      Interessen

180 DEVELOPMENT FACTOR
    f Facteur de développement
    d Entwicklungsfaktor

181 SPATIAL FACTOR
    f Facteur spatial
    d Raumfaktor

182 FIELDS IN ECONOMICS
    f Domaines économiques
    d Wirtschaftliche Gebiete

183 FORCES OF PROGRESS
    f Forces du progrès
    d Kräfte des Fortschritts

184 ECONOMIC FRAMEWORK
    f Cadre économique
    d Wirtschaftlicher Rahmen

185 GAP
    f Décalage
    d Kluft;
      Abstand

186 GAP IN PER CAPITA
    INCOME
    f Décalage des revenus
      par habitant
    d Diskrepanz im per capita
      Einkommen

187 ECONOMIC GEOGRAPHY
    f Géographie économique
    d Wirtschaftsgeographie

209 NATIONALISM
   f  Nationalisme
   d  Nationalismus

210 TWIN NATIONS
   f  Nations jumelles
   d  Nachbarnationen

211 NEED FOR ASSISTANCE
   f  Besoins d'assistance
   d  Unterstützungsbedarf

212 FELT NEEDS
   f  Fausses priorités
   d  Eingebildete Bedürfnisse

213 REAL NEEDS
   f  Besoins réels
   d  Echte Bedürfnisse

214 NON-ALIGNMENT
   f  Non-alignement
   d  Bündnisfreiheit

215 NON-DISCRIMINATION
   f  Non-discrimination
   d  Nicht-Diskriminierung

216 ONE-CROP PRODUCTION
   f  Mono-production
   d  Monoproduktion

217 OUTPUT
   f  Production
   d  Produktion;
      Output

218 PARTNERSHIP
   f  Association;
      Partnership
   d  Partnerschaft

219 PEACE CORPS
   f  Corps de la paix
   d  Friedenskorps

220 PILOT COLONY
   f  Colonie pilote
   d  Modellkolonie

221 FOREIGN POLICY
   f  Politique extérieure
   d  Aussenpolitik

222 PRIMARY PRODUCERS
   f  Producteurs de matières
      premières
   d  Basisgüter-Produzenten

223 PRIMARY PRODUCT
   f  Produit de base
   d  Basisprodukt

224 ECONOMIC PROGRESS
   f  Progrès économique
   d  Wirtschaftlicher
      Fortschritt

225 SOCIAL PROGRESS
   f  Progrès social
   d  Sozialer Fortschritt

226 TECHNICAL PROGRESS
   f  Progrès technique
   d  Technischer Fortschritt

227 PROMOTION OF ECONOMIC
     DEVELOPMENT
   f  Encouragement de
      l'économie
   d  Wirtschaftsförderung

228 PROPERTY RIGHTS
   f  Droits de propriété
   d  Eigentumsrechte

229 PUBLIC RELATIONS
   f  Relations publics
   d  Öffentlichkeitsarbeit

230 REGION OF OPTIMUM
     DEVELOPMENT
   f  Région de développement
      optimum
   d  Region der optimalen
      Entwicklung

231 RUBLE OFFENSIVE
   f  Offensive de rouble
   d  Rubeloffensive

232 SELF-DETERMINATION
  f   Auto-détermination
  d   Selbstbestimmung

233 SELF-HELP
  f   Effort local de développe-
      ment;
      Efforts propres;
      Selfhelp
  d   Selbsthilfe

234 SELF-HELP INSTITUTIONS
  f   Institutions locales de
      développement;
      Institutions de selfhelp
  d   Selbsthilfe-Einrichtungen

235 COOPERATIVE SELF-HELP
  f   Selfhelp coopératif;
      Efforts propres des
      coopératives
  d   Genossenschaftliche
      Selbsthilfe

236 SELF-SUFFICIENCY
  f   Autarcie
  d   Autarkie

237 AUXILIARY TECHNICAL
    SERVICES
  f   Service technique
      auxiliaire
  d   Technische Hilfsein-
      richtungen

238 TECHNICAL SHORT-
    COMINGS
  f   Lacunes techniques
  d   Technische Mängel

239 SOCIAL OVERHEAD
    CAPITAL (S.O.C.);
    HIRSCHMAN
  f   Infrastructure écono-
      mique et sociale (I.E.S.)
  d   Sozio-ökonomische
      Infrastruktur

240 AFRICAN SOCIALISM
  f   Socialisme africain
  d   Afrikanischer Sozia-
      lismus

241 AGRARIAN SOCIALISM
  f   Socialisme agraire
  d   Agrarsozialismus

242 STABILIZATION POLICY
  f   Politique de stabilisation
  d   Stabilisierungspolitik

243 STANDARD OF LIVING
  f   Niveau de vie
  d   Lebensstandard

244 SURPLUS
  f   Excédents;
      Surplus
  d   Überschüsse

245 TAKE OFF;
    ROSTOW
  f   Décollage;
      Démarrage
  d   Aufschwung

246 OVERALL TARGETS
  f   Objectifs globaux
  d   Gesamtziele

247 TECHNOLOGICAL DEFICIT
  f   Déficit technologique
  d   Technologisches Defizit

248 OPTIMUM USE
  f   Utilisation optimum
  d   Optimale Benützung

249 PUBLIC UTILITIES;
    PUBLIC SERVICES
  f   Services publics
  d   Öffentliche Dienst-
      leistungen

250 VALUE ADDED
  f   Valeur ajoutée
  d   Mehrwert

251 VERSATILE TEAM
  f   Equipe polyvalente
  d   Polyvalentes Team

252 WESTERNIZATION
  f   Occidentalisation
  d   Verwestlichung

253   WORKING PARTY
      f   Groupe de travail
      d   Arbeitsgruppe

254   PUBLIC WORKS
      f   Travaux publics
      d   Öffentliche Arbeiten

255   WORLD III;
      THIRD WORLD
      f   Tiers Monde
      d   Dritte Welt

# II.
# PLANNING
# PLANIFICATION
# PLANUNG

274 COMPENSATION
   f  Indemnisation
   d  Entschädigung

275 ECONOMIC
   CONCENTRATION
   f  Concentration économique
   d  Wirtschaftliche Konzen-
      tration

276 URBAN CONCENTRATION
   f  Concentration urbaine
   d  Städtische Konzentration

277 CONSISTENCY TEST
   f  Test de cohérence
   d  Konsistenztest

278 APPARENT CONSUMPTION
   f  Consommation apparente
   d  Scheinbarer Konsum

279 FINAL CONSUMPTION
   f  Consommation finale
   d  Endkonsum

280 INTERMEDIATE CONSUMP-
   TION
   f  Consommation intermé-
      diaire
   d  Zwischenkonsum

281 PER CAPITA CONSUMP-
   TION
   f  Consommation par
      habitant
   d  Per capita Konsum

282 REAL CONSUMPTION
   f  Consommation réelle
   d  Realer Konsum

283 COOPERATION ORGANI-
   ZATION
   f  Organisation coopérative
   d  Kooperative Organisation

284 COOPERATION PRO-
   GRAMMES
   f  Programmes de coopéra-
      tion
   d  Kooperationsprogramme

285 ECONOMIC COOPERATION
   f  Coopération économique
   d  Wirtschaftliche Koopera-
      tion

286 INTER-TERRITORIAL
   COOPERATION
   f  Coopération interterri-
      toriale
   d  Interterritoriale
      Kooperation

287 INTRA-AFRICAN
   COOPERATION
   f  Coopération interafricaine
   d  Interafrikanische
      Kooperation

288 MUTUAL COOPERATION
   f  Coopération mutuelle
   d  Gegenseitige Kooperation

289 TECHNICAL COOPERATION
   f  Coopération technique
   d  Technische Kooperation

290 REGIONAL COOPERATION
   f  Coopération régionale
   d  Regionale Kooperation

291 AGREEMENT ON ECONO-
   MIC COOPÈRATION
   f  Accord de coopération
      économique
   d  Abkommen über wirt-
      schaftliche Kooperation

292 COORDINATION
   COMMITTEE
   f  Comité de coordination
   d  Koordinationsausschuss

293 COORDINATION OF
   ECONOMIC INTERESTS
   f  Coordination des intérêts
      économiques
   d  Wirtschaftliche Interessen-
      abstimmung

294 GLOBAL COORDINATION
   f  Coordination planétaire
   d  Globale Koordination

295 MAXIMUM COORDINATION
   f  Maximum de coordination
   d  Maximale Koordination

296 TECHNICAL
   COORDINATION
   f  Coordination technique
   d  Technische Koordination

297 METHODS OF
   COORDINATION
   f  Méthodes de coordination
   d  Koordinationsmethoden

298 QUASI-GOVERNMENTAL
   CORPORATION
   f  Organisation para-éta-
      tique;
      Organisation gouverne-
      mentale
   d  Halbstaatliche Organisa-
      tion

299 COMMERCIAL PROFITABI-
   LITY CRITERION
   f  Critère de la rentabilité
      commerciale
   d  Rentabilitätskriterium

300 FACTOR INTENSITY
   CRITERION
   f  Critère de l'intensité
      des facteurs
   d  Faktorintensitätskrite-
      rium

301 NATIONAL ECONOMIC
   PROFITABILITY CRITERION
   f  Critère de rentabilité du
      point de vue de l'économie
      nationale
   d  Nationalwirtschaftliches
      Rentabilitätskriterium

302 CONSUMER DEMAND
   f  Demande de consommation
   d  Konsumnachfrage

303 INVESTMENT DEMAND
   f  Demande d'investissement
   d  Investitionsnachfrage

304 DUPLICATION
   f  Double emploi
   d  Zweigleisigkeit

305 BACKWARD ECONOMY
   f  Economie arriérée
   d  Unterentwickelte
      Wirtschaft

306 COLLECTIVE ECONOMY;
   PLANNED ECONOMY
   f  Economie planifiée;
      Dirigisme
   d  Planwirtschaft

307 CAPITALISTIC ECONOMY
   f  Economie capitaliste
   d  Kapitalistische Wirtschaft

308 OVERALL ECONOMY
   f  Economie générale
   d  Gesamtwirtschaft

309 SOCIALIST ECONOMY
   f  Economie socialiste
   d  Sozialistische Wirtschaft

310 BRANCH OF THE ECONOMY
   f  Branche économique
   d  Wirtschaftszweig

311 PILLAR OF ECONOMY
   f  Pilier de l'économie
   d  Wirtschaftsträger

312 FRONTIER EFFECTS
   f  Effets frontières
   d  Grenzeffekte

313 SIDE EFFECTS
   f  Effets secondaires
   d  Nebenwirkungen

314 STATE ENTERPRISE
   f  Entreprise étatique
   d  Staatliches Unternehmen

315 EVALUATION PROCEDURES
   f  Méthodes d'évaluation
   d  Bewertungsverfahren

316 EXCHANGE OF
EXPERIENCES
f   Echange d'expériences
d   Erfahrungsaustausch

317 EXPECTATIONS
f   Prévisions;
Espérances
d   Erwartungen

318 EXPERT ADVICE
f   Expertise
d   Gutachten

319 EXPROPRIATION
f   Expropriation
d   Enteignung

320 FACTOR OF PRODUCTION
f   Facteur de production
d   Produktionsfaktor

321 ECONOMIC FACTOR
f   Facteur économique
d   Wirtschaftlicher Faktor

322 KEY FACTOR
f   Facteur clé
d   Schlüsselfaktor

323 PRODUCTIVITY FACTOR
f   Facteur de productivité
d   Produktivitätsfaktor

324 FEASIBILITY
f   Viabilité;
Feasibility
d   Feasibility;
Durchführbarkeit

325 FEASIBILITY STUDY
f   Etude sur les possibilités
de réalisation
d   Feasibility Untersuchung;
Aktenstudium;
Durchführbarkeitsstudie

326 FEED-BACK CONTROL
f   Feed-back contrôle
d   Feed-back Kontrolle

327 FLUCTUATIONS
f   Fluctuations
d   Schwankungen

328 FOLLOW-UP
f   Follow-up
d   Nachbetreuung;
Nachkontakte

329 PRODUCTIVE FORCES
f   Forces productives
d   Produktive Kräfte

330 GESTATION PERIOD
f   Période de maturation
d   Reifungsperiode

331 LOCAL GOVERNMENT
f   Gouvernement local
d   Lokale Regierung

332 GOVERNMENTAL ACTION
f   Action gouvernementale
d   Regierungsaktion

333 GOVERNMENTAL
PRIORITIES
f   Priorités gouvernemen-
tales
d   Regierungsprioritäten

334 BALANCED GROWTH
f   Croissance équilibrée
d   Ausgeglichenes Wachs-
tum

335 CONSISTENT GROWTH
f   Croissance cohérente
d   Konsistentes Wachstum

336 EVEN GROWTH
f   Croissance équilibrée
d   Gleichgewichtiges
Wachstum

337 IMMISERIZING GROWTH;
BHAGWATI
f   Croissance décroissante;
Croissance négative
d   Negatives Wachstum

338 HARMONIZED GROWTH
  f  Croissance harmonisée
  d  Harmonisiertes Wachstum

339 SELF-SUSTAINED GROWTH;
  ROSTOW
  f  Croissance continue;
     Croissance auto-entre-
     tenue
  d  Autonomes Wachstum;
     Selbsttragendes Wachstum

340 SLOW GROWTH
  f  Lente expansion
  d  Mässiges Wachstum

341 SUSTAINED GROWTH
  f  Expansion suivie
  d  Kontinuierliches Wachstum

342 UNBALANCED GROWTH
  SEQUENCE;
  HIRSCHMAN
  f  Séquence de croissance
     non-équilibrée
  d  Inbalanzierte Wachstums-
     sequenz

343 ANNUAL RATE OF GROWTH
  f  Taux annuel de croissance
  d  Jährliche Wachstumsrate

344 COROLLARY OF ECONOMIC
  GROWTH
  f  Corollaire de l'expansion
     économique;
     Effets de croissance
  d  Wachstumseffekte

345 PROBLEMS OF GROWTH
  f  Problèmes de croissance
  d  Wachstumsprobleme

346 THEORY OF ECONOMIC
  GROWTH
  f  Théorie de croissance
  d  Wachstumstheorie

347 IMPLEMENTATION OF
  THE PLAN
  f  Exécution du plan;
     Mise en oeuvre du plan
  d  Durchführung des Planes

348 INSTALLATION PERIOD
  f  Période d'installation
  d  Installationsperiode

349 PARA-PUBLIC INSTITUTE
  f  Para-public institut
  d  Halbstaatliches Institut

350 INTEGRATION METHODS
  f  Méthodes d'intégration
  d  Integrationsmethoden

351 ECONOMIC INTEGRATION
  f  Intégration économique
  d  Wirtschaftliche Integration

352 INTERNATIONAL INTEGRA-
  TION
  f  Intégration internationale
  d  Internationale Integration

353 REGIONAL INTEGRATION
  f  Intégration régionale
  d  Regionale Integration

354 LINES OF INTEGRATION
  f  Lignes de l'intégration
  d  Integrationslinien

355 KEY RESOURCES
  f  Ressources de base
  d  Basisreserven

356 LEADING SECTOR;
  ROSTOW
  f  Secteur moteur
  d  Führender Sektor

357 LIAISON OFFICER
  f  Chargé de liaison
  d  Verbindungsbeamter

381 ECONOMIC PLAN
    f   Plan économique
    d  Ökonomischer Plan

382 GLOBAL PLAN
    f   Plan global
    d  Gesamtplan

383 NATIONAL PLAN
    f   Plan national
    d  Nationaler Plan

384 NORMATIVE PLAN
    f   Plan normatif
    d  Normativer Plan;
       Normplan

385 PROSPECTIVE PLAN
    f   Plan perspectif
    d  Perspektiver Plan

386 REHABILITATION PLAN
    f   Plan d'assainissement
    d  Sanierungsplan

387 SECTORIAL PLAN
    f   Plan sectoriel
    d  Sektorieller Plan;
       Sektorenplan

388 STABILIZATION PLAN
    f   Plan de stabilisation
    d  Stabilisierungsplan

389 REORIENTATION OF THE
    PLAN
    f   Réorientation du plan
    d  Neuorientierung des
       Planes;
       Umorientierung des
       Planes

390 TEXT OF PLANS
    f   Texte des plans
    d  Planungstext

391 UPDATING OF PLAN
    f   Actualisation du plan
    d  Aktualisierung des Planes

392 PLANNER
    f   Planificateur
    d  Planer

393 PLANNING ACTIVITY
    f   Activité planificative
    d  Planungstätigkeit

394 PLANNING AGENCY;
    PLANNING AUTHORITY;
    PLANNING BOARD
    f   Organisme de la
       planification
    d  Planungsbehörde

395 PLANNING COMMISSION
    f   Commission de
       planification
    d  Planungskommission

396 PLANNING COMMITTEE
    f   Comité de planification
    d  Planungsausschuss

397 PLANNING DEPARTMENT
    f   Service du plan
    d  Planungsabteilung

398 PLANNING OF DEVELOP-
    MENT AID
    f   Planification de l'aide
       au développement
    d  Planung der Entwicklungs-
       hilfe

399 PLANNING EXPERIENCES
    f   Expériences de planifi-
       cation
    d  Planungserfahrungen

400 PLANNING FETISHISM
    f   Fétichisme du plan
    d  Planungsfetischismus

401 PLANNING INSTITUTIONS;
    PLANNING SERVICES
    f   Institutions de planifi-
       cation
    d  Planungsinstitutionen

402 PLANNING METHODS
   f  Méthodes de planification
   d  Planungsmethoden

403 PLANNING MODELS
   f  Modèles de planification
   d  Planungsmodelle

404 PLANNING OFFICER
   f  Agent de planification
   d  Planungsbeamter

405 PLANNING ORGANIZATION
   f  Appareil de planification
   d  Planungsapparat

406 PLANNING POSSIBILITIES
   f  Possibilités d'aménage-
      ments
   d  Planungsmöglichkeiten

407 PLANNING PROBLEMS
   f  Problèmes de planifica-
      tion
   d  Planungsprobleme

408 PLANNING PROJECTS
   f  Projets de planification
   d  Planungsprojekte

409 PLANNING RESEARCH
   f  Recherches de planifi-
      cation
   d  Planungsforschung

410 PLANNING SERVICES
   f  Services de la
      planification
   d  Planungsdienste

411 PLANNING IN STAGES;
   TINBERGEN
   f  Planification par étapes
   d  Planung in Etappen

412 PLANNING STANDARDS
   f  Normes de la planification
   d  Planungsstandard

413 PLANNING SYSTEM
   f  Système de planification
   d  Planungssystem

414 PLANNING TARGETS
   f  Objectifs du plan
   d  Planungsziele

415 PLANNING TECHNIQUES
   f  Techniques de planification
   d  Planungstechnik

416 PLANNING UNIT
   f  Unité de planification
   d  Planungseinheit

417 APPLIED PLANNING
   f  Planification appliquée
   d  Angewandte Planung

418 CENTRAL PLANNING;
   TINBERGEN
   f  Planification centralisée
   d  Zentrales Planen

419 COLONIAL PLANNING
   f  Planification coloniale
   d  Koloniale Planung

420 COMPREHENSIVE PLANNING
   f  Planification intégrale
   d  Integrale Planung

421 DEVELOPMENT PLANNING
   f  Planification du développe-
      ment
   d  Entwicklungsplanung

422 DYNAMIC PLANNING
   f  Planification dynamique
   d  Dynamisches Planen

423 ECONOMIC PLANNING
   f  Planification économique
   d  Wirtschaftsplanung

424 HEALTH PLANNING
   f  Politique de la santé
   d  Gesundheitsplanung

425 IMPERATIVE PLANNING
   f  Planification impérative
   d  Imperatives Planen

25

426 INCOME PLANNING
f  Planification des revenus
d  Einkommensplanung

427 INDICATIVE PLANNING
f  Planification indicative
d  Indikative Planung

428 INTERREGIONAL PLANNING
f  Planification interrégionale
d  Interregionale Planung

429 LONG-TERM PLANNING
f  Planification à long terme
d  Langfristige Planung

430 NATIONAL PLANNING
f  Planification nationale
d  Nationale Planung

431 OPERATIONAL PLANNING
f  Planification fonctionnelle
d  Funktionelle Planung

432 OVERALL PLANNING
f  Planification globale
d  Gesamtplanung

433 SPATIAL ECONOMICS;
   "PHYSICAL PLANNING"
f  Planification de l'espace;
   Aménagement de l'espace
d  Raumplanung

434 REGIONAL PLANNING
f  Planification régionale
d  Regionale Planung

435 TOWN PLANNING
f  Aménagement urbain
d  Städteplanung

436 WATER PLANNING
f  Planification des eaux
d  Wasserplanung

437 FLEXIBLE SYSTEM OF
   PLANNING
f  Planification souple
d  Flexibeles System der
   Planung

438 ORGANIZATIONAL FRAME-
   WORK OF PLANNING
f  Organisation de planification
d  Planungsorganisation

439 PRECONDITIONS;
   PREREQUISITES
f  Conditions préalables
d  Vorbedingungen

440 PRIORITY STANDARDS
f  Normes de priorité
d  Prioritätsstandard

441 PROBLEMS OF ASSOCIATION
f  Problèmes d'association
d  Assoziierungsprobleme

442 ADMINISTRATIVE
   PROBLEMS
f  Problèmes administratifs
d  Administrative Probleme;
   Verwaltungsprobleme

443 LOCAL PRODUCE
f  Produit local
d  Lokales Produkt

444 PRODUCTION CONDITIONS
f  Conditions de production
d  Produktionsbedingungen

445 PRODUCTION COSTS
f  Coûts de production
d  Produktionskosten

446 PRODUCTION FORECAST
f  Prévision de production
d  Produktionsplanung

447 PRODUCTION INSTRUMENT
f  Instrument de production
d  Produktionsinstrument

448 PRODUCTION TECHNIQUES
f  Méthodes de production
d  Produktionstechnik

449 PRODUCTION UNIT
f  Unité de production
d  Produktionseinheit

d  Partizipationsprogramm

470  PROJECT EVALUATION
f  Evaluation des projets
d  Projektbeurteilung

471  PROJECT EXECUTION
f  Exécution du projet;
   Mise en oeuvre du projet
d  Projektausführung

472  PROJECT HISTORY
f  Histoire du projet
d  Projektdarstellung

473  CONSTRUCTION PROJECT
f  Projet de construction
d  Konstruktionsprojekt

474  INTEGRATED PROJECT
f  Projet intégré
d  Integriertes Projekt

475  KEY PROJECT
f  Projet clef
d  Schlüsselprojekt

476  LARGE PROJECT
f  Grand projet
d  Schwerpunktprojekt

477  PILOT PROJECT
f  Projet pilote
d  Pionierprojekt

478  PROJECT BY PROJECT
APPROACH
f  Approche projet par
   projet
d  Projektmethode

479  STUDY PROJECT
f  Etude de projet
d  Projektstudie

480  TURNKEY PROJECT
f  Projet «clef en mains»
d  Zentralprojekt

481  "WHITE ELEPHANT
PROJECT"
f  Projet non-rentable
d  Projekt "weisser Ele-
   phant"

482  PROJECTION METHODS
f  Méthodes de projection
d  Projektionsmethoden

483  PROJECTION OF DEMAND
f  Projection de la demande
d  Nachfrage-Projektion

484  ECONOMIC PROJECTION
f  Projection économique
d  Wirtschaftliche Projektion

485  MARGINAL PROPENSITY
TO CONSUME
f  Propension marginale à
   consommer
d  Marginale Grenzneigung
   des Konsums

486  RATE OF RETURN
f  Taux de rentabilité
d  Rentabilitätsrate

487  RATIONALIZATION
MEASURES
f  Mesures de rationalisation
d  Rationalisierungsmass-
   nahmen

488  STRATEGIC RAW MATERIAL
f  Matière première
   stratégique
d  Strategisches Rohmaterial

489  REGIONAL AGREEMENT
f  Entente régionale;
   Accord régional
d  Regionalabkommen

490  REGIONAL ANALYSIS
f  Analyse régionale
d  Regionalanalyse

491 REGIONAL BODIES
  f Organes régionaux
  d Regionalbehörden

492 REGIONAL CENTRE
  f Centre régional
  d Regionalzentrum

493 REGIONAL DEVELOPMENT
  f Développement régional
  d Regionalentwicklung

494 REGIONAL ECONOMICS
  f Economie régionale
  d Regionalwirtschaft

495 REGIONAL LEVEL
  f Niveau régional
  d Regionalebene

496 REGIONAL ORGANIZATIONS
  f Organisations régionales
  d Regionalorganisationen

497 RESOURCE SURVEY
  f Inventaire des ressources
  d Inventar der Reserven

498 NATURAL RESOURCES
  f Richesses naturelles
  d Natürlicher Reichtum

499 POTENTIAL RESOURCES
  f Ressources potentielles
  d Potentieller Reichtum

500 SCARCITY OF RESOURCES
  f Rareté des ressources
  d Mangel an Mitteln

501 RESTRICTIVE MEASURE
  f Mesure restrictive
  d Restriktive Massnahmen

502 LEADING SECTOR
  f Secteur entraînant;
    Secteur moteur
  d Führender Sektor

503 MODERN SECTOR
  f Secteur moderne
  d Moderner Sektor

504 PRIMARY SECTOR;
    SECONDARY SECTOR;
    TERTIARY SECTOR
  f Secteur primaire;
    Secteur secondaire;
    Secteur tertiaire
  d Primärer Sektor;
    Sekundärer Sektor;
    Tertiärer Sektor

505 PRIVATE SECTOR
  f Secteur privé
  d Privater Sektor

506 PRODUCTIVE SECTOR
  f Secteur productif
  d Produktiver Sektor

507 PUBLIC SECTOR
  f Secteur public
  d Öffentlicher Sektor

508 STATE SECTOR
  f Secteur étatique;
    Secteur public
  d Staatlicher Sektor

509 SECTORAL DISTRIBUTION
  f Répartition sectorielle
  d Sektorielle Verteilung

510 SENIOR CIVIL SERVANTS
  f Cadres administratifs
  d Höhere Beamte

511 CIVIL SERVICE
  f Fonction publique;
    Service civique
  d Staatsdienst

512 PERIOD OF STAGNATION
  f Période de stagnation
  d Stagnationsperiode

513 STATE CONTROL
  f Contrôle de l'Etat;
    Mainmise de l'Etat
  d Staatskontrolle

514 ECONOMIC STIMULANTS
  f Stimulants économiques

d Wirtschaftliche
Incentives;
Wirtschaftsstimulatoren

515 STRUCTURAL ASSISTANCE
f Aide aux structures
d Strukturhilfe

516 STRUCTURAL DEFICIENCY
f Déficience de structure
d Strukturmangel

517 STRUCTURAL REFORMS
f Réformes des structures
d Strukturreformen

518 STRUCTURAL TRANSFOR-
MATION
f Transformation structu-
rale
d Strukturtransformation

519 DUALISTIC STRUCTURE
f Structure dualiste
d Dualistische Struktur

520 ECONOMIC STRUCTURE
f Structure économique
d Ökonomische Struktur

521 TRADITIONAL STRUCTURE
f Structure traditionnelle
d Traditionelle Struktur

522 SECTORIAL STRUCTURE
f Structure sectorielle
d Sektorielle Struktur

523 ECONOMIC STRATEGY
f Stratégie économique
d Wirtschaftliche Strategie

524 GLOBAL STRATEGY
f Stratégie globale
d Globalstrategie

525 MINIMUM OF SUBSISTENCE
f Minimum vital
d Existenzminimum

526 POSSIBILITIES OF
SUBSTITUTION
f Possibilités de substitution
d Substitutionsmöglich-
keiten

527 TRANSFER OF FUNCTIONS
f Transfert des pouvoirs
d Übertragung der
Funktionen

528 PRIORITY UNDERTAKING
f Entreprise prioritaire
d Prioritätsunternehmen

529 VICIOUS CIRCLE OF
POVERTY;
NURKSE, MYRDAL
f Cercle vicieux de la
pauvreté
d Viziöser Kreis der
Armut

530 WELFARE STATE
f Etat-providence
d Wohlfahrtsstaat

# III.

## AGRICULTURE
## AGRICULTURE
## LANDWIRTSCHAFT

531 AGRARIAN LEGISLATION;
LAND LAWS
f  Législation agraire
d  Agrarische Gesetzgebung;
Agrargesetzgebung

532 AGRARIAN REFORM;
LAND REFORM
f  Réforme agraire
d  Agrarreform

533 AGRICULTURAL ACCOUN-
TING
f  Comptabilité agricole
d  Landwirtschaftliche
Buchhaltung

534 AGRICULTURAL ADVISORY
SCHEME
f  Animation rurale
d  Landwirtschaftliches
Beratungswesen

535 AGRICULTURAL
COOPERATIVES
f  Coopératives agricoles
d  Landwirtschaftliche
Genossenschaften

536 AGRICULTURAL CREDIT
f  Crédit agricole
d  Agrarkredit

537 AGRICULTURAL DEVELOP-
MENT
f  Développement de
l'agriculture
d  Entwicklung der Land-
wirtschaft

538 AGRICULTURAL
ECONOMICS
f  Economie agricole
d  Agrarwirtschaft

539 AGRICULTURAL ENGINEER
f  Ingénieur agronome
d  Diplomlandwirt

540 AGRICULTURAL ENGINEE-
RING
f  Génie rural
d  Agrartechnik

541 AGRICULTURAL EXTENSION
CENTRE
f  Centre de vulgarisation
agricole
d  Landwirtschaftliches
Fortbildungszentrum

542 AGRICULTURAL LAW
f  Législation rurale;
Lois agraires
d  Agrarrecht;
Agrargesetze

543 AGRICULTURAL MACHINE-
RY
f  Machines agricoles
d  Landwirtschaftliche
Maschinen

544 AGRICULTURAL MARKET
f  Marché agricole
d  Agrarmarkt

545 AGRICULTURAL
PLANNING
f  Planification agricole
d  Agrarplanung

546 AGRICULTURAL POLICY
f  Politique agricole
d  Agrarpolitik

547 AGRICULTURAL PROCES-
SING INDUSTRY
f Transformation de pro-
duits agricoles
d Verarbeitung landwirt-
schaftlicher Produkte

548 AGRICULTURAL PRODUCE;
FARM PRODUCTS
f Produits agricoles
d Landwirtschaftliche
Produkte

549 AGRICULTURAL PRODUC-
TION
f Production agricole
d Agrarproduktion

550 AGRICULTURAL PRODUCTS
f Denrées agricoles
d Agrarprodukte

551 AGRICULTURAL
PROTECTIONISM
f Protectionnisme agricole
d Agrarprotektionismus

552 AGRONOMIC RESEARCH
f Recherche agronomique
d Agronomische Forschung

553 AGRICULTURAL SECTOR
f Secteur agricole
d Agrarsektor

554 AGRICULTURAL SERVICES
f Vulgarisation agricole
d Landwirtschaftliche
Vulgarisation

555 AGRICULTURAL UNIT
f Unité culturale
d Bebauungseinheit

556 MECHANIZED AGRICUL-
TURE
f Agriculture mécanisée
d Mechanisierte Landwirt-
schaft

557 TROPICAL AGRICULTURE
f Agriculture tropicale
d Tropische Landwirtschaft

558 AGRONOMIZATION
f Agronomisation
d Agronomisierung

559 TROPICAL AGRONOMY
f Agronomie tropicale
d Tropische Agronomie

560 RURAL ANIMATION
f Animation rurale
d Animation der ländlichen
Gebiete

561 ANIMAL PRODUCTION;
ANIMAL HUSBANDRY;
LIVESTOCK RAISING;
LIVESTOCK BREEDING
f Elevage du bétail;
Production animale
d Tierzucht;
Viehzucht

562 ARBORICULTURE
f Arboriculture
d Baumkultur

563 UTILIZABLE AREA
f Surface utilisable
d Bebaubare Fläche

564 BANANAS
f Bananes
d Bananen

565 BANANA CULTIVATION
f Bananculture
d Bananenkultur

566 BANANA PLANTATION
f Bananeraie
d Bananenpflanzung

567 BANANA TREE
f Bananier
d Bananenstrauch

568 BEEKEEPING
  f  Apiculture
  d  Bienenzucht

569 BOVIDAE
  f  Bovidés
  d  Boviden

570 CROSS-BREEDING
  f  Croisements
  d  Kreuzungen

571 "FREEDOM FROM HUNGER"
  CAMPAIGN
  f  Campagne mondiale
     contre la faim
  d  Weltkampagne gegen den
     Hunger

572 CAPACITY OF THE EARTH
  CARRYING
  f  Capacité de peuplement
     de la terre
  d  Ernährungsfähigkeit des
     Bodens

573 CASHEW-NUT
  f  Anacarde;
     Noix d'acajou
  d  Kaschunuss

574 CATTLE MANAGEMENT
  f  Organisation du bétail
  d  Tierverwaltung

575 TRAINING CENTRE FOR
  CATTLE-REARING
  f  Centre de formation pour
     l'élevage du bétail
  d  Tierzuchtlehrbetrieb

576 CENTRE OF RURAL
  EXPANSION
  f  Centre d'expansion
     rurale (C.E.R.)
  d  Ländliches Expansions-
     zentrum

577 CEREALS
  f  Céréales
  d  Getreide

578 CITRICULTURE
  f  Culture des agrumes
  d  Agrumenkultur

579 CLIMATE
  f  Climat
  d  Klima

580 CLIMATIC HAZARDS
  f  Aléas climatiques
  d  Klimatische Risken

581 COCOA
  f  Cacao
  d  Kakao

582 COCONUT
  f  Noix de coco
  d  Kokosnuss

583 COFFEE GROWING
  f  Culture du café
  d  Kaffeeanbau

584 COFFEE TREE
  f  Caféier
  d  Kaffeestrauch

585 COPRA
  f  Copra
  d  Kopra

586 COTTON CROPS
  f  Cultures de coton
  d  Baumwollkulturen

587 COTTON SEEDS
  f  Graines de coton
  d  Baumwollsamen

588 CROP DIVERSIFICATION
  f  Diversification des
     cultures
  d  Diversifikation der
     Kulturen

589 CROP GRADING
  f  Classement des produits
     agricoles
  d  Klassifikation der
     Agrarprodukte

590 CROP PROTECTION;
PLANT PROTECTION
f   Protection des cultures
d   Pflanzenschutz

591 CROP ROTATION
f   Rotation des cultures
d   Fruchtwechsel;
Fruchtfolge

592 BASIC CROPS
f   Cultures de base
d   Basiskulturen

593 BUSH CROPS
f   Produits de la brousse
d   Buschprodukte

594 FODDER CROP
f   Fourrage
d   Viehfutter

595 INDUSTRIAL CROPS
f   Cultures industrielles
d   Industriekulturen

596 TROPICAL CROPS
f   Cultures de la zone
tropicale
d   Tropische Kulturen

597 CULTIVATION;
FARMING
f   Exploitation
d   Bewirtschaftung

598 FIELD AND OPEN CROP
CULTIVATION
f   Cultures spéciales
d   Spezialkulturen

599 CULTIVATION TECHNIQUES
f   Techniques culturales
d   Bewirtschaftungstechnik

600 CULTIVATION OF VEGE-
TABLES
f   Culture maraîchère
d   Gemüsebau

601 DAIRY INDUSTRY
f   Industrie laitière
d   Molkereiwesen

602 DAIRY ENGINEERING
f   Technique laitière
d   Milchverarbeitungstechnik

603 DEMONSTRATION PLOT
f   Parcelle témoin
d   Landwirtschaftliche
Demonstrationszelle

604 EXTENSION OF THE
DESERT
f   Extension du désert
d   Vordringen der Wüste

605 COMMUNITY DEVELOP-
MENT
f   Développement des
communautés rurales
d   Entwicklung der länd-
lichen Siedlungen

606 RURAL DEVELOPMENT
f   Aménagement rural
d   Entwicklung der länd-
lichen Gebiete

607 DRAINAGE
f   Drainage
d   Entwässerung;
Drainage

608 DROUGHT
f   Sécheresse
d   Trockenheit

609 DRYING THE CROP
f   Séchage
d   Abtrocknung;
Trocknung

610 EROSION MANAGEMENT
f   Lutte contre l'érosion
d   Erosionsbekämpfung

611 EQUIDAE
f   Equidés
d   Equiden

612 REAL ESTATE
EVALUATION
f  Estimation des biens
   fonciers
d  Evaluation des Grund-
   besitzes

613 COOPERATIVE EXPERT
f  Expert en coopération
d  Experte für das
   Genossenschaftswesen

614 DAIRY EXPERT
f  Expert de l'industrie
   laitière
d  Experte der Milch-
   industrie

615 FORESTRY EXPERT
f  Spécialiste de sylvi-
   culture
d  Forstexperte

616 IRRIGATION EXPERT
f  Expert en irrigation
d  Bewässerungsexperte

617 MARITIME FISHING EX-
PERT
f  Spécialiste de la pêche
   en mer
d  Experte für Meeresfisch-
   fang;
   Experte für Hochsee-
   fischerei

618 NUTRITION EXPERT
f  Consultant en matière
   nutrition
d  Experte für Nahrungs-
   probleme

619 EXTENSION AGENT
f  Agent agricole;
   Moniteur agricole
d  Entwicklungshelfer im
   Agrarsektor

620 EXTENSION WORKER
f  Vulgarisateur
d  Vulgarisateur

621 FARM
f  Exploitation agricole;
   Ferme
d  Farm

622 FARM ADMINISTRATION
f  Gestion des exploitations
   agricoles
d  Verwaltung der landwirt-
   schaftlichen Unternehmen

623 FARM BUILDINGS
f  Construction rurale
d  Landwirtschaftliches
   Bauwesen

624 FARM EQUIPMENT
f  Equipement agricole
d  Farmausstattung

625 FARM IMPLEMENTS
f  Outils agricoles
d  Landwirtschaftliche
   Geräte

626 FARM MANAGEMENT
f  Gestion des exploitations
   agricoles
d  Farmverwaltung

627 FAMILY FARM
f  Exploitation familiale
d  Landwirtschaftlicher
   Familienbetrieb

628 LARGE FARM;
LARGE PLANTATION
f  Grande exploitation
d  Grossbetrieb

629 MEDIUM-SIZE FARM
f  Exploitation moyenne
d  Mittelbetrieb

630 PILOT FARM
f  Ferme pilote
d  Musterbetrieb

631 SMALL FARM;
SMALL HOLDING
f  Petite exploitation;
   Micro-fundium
d  Kleinbetrieb

632 VILLAGE FARM
    f  Exploitation villageoise
    d  Landwirtschaftlicher
       Dorfbetrieb

633 FARMING EQUIPMENT;
    AGRICULTURAL EQUIP-
    MENT
    f  Matériel agricole
    d  Landwirtschaftliche
       Geräte

634 FARMING METHODS
    f  Méthodes culturales
    d  Bewirtschaftungsmethoden

635 CROP FARMING
    f  Culture des plantes
    d  Pflanzenbau

636 DRY FARMING
    f  Dry farming;
       Culture à sec
    d  Trockenkulturen

637 EXTENSIVE FARMING
    f  Culture extensive
    d  Extensive Bodenbewirt-
       schaftung

638 INTENSIVE FARMING
    f  Culture intensive
    d  Intensive Bodenbewirt-
       schaftung

639 POULTRY FARMING;
    POULTRY KEEPING;
    POULTRY RAISING
    f  Aviculture
    d  Geflügelzucht

640 SINGLE-CROP FARMING
    f  Monoculture
    d  Monokultur

641 SUBSISTENCE FARMING
    f  Production agricole du
       subsistance
    d  Landwirtschaftliche
       Subsistenzproduktion

642 FATS
    f  Corps gras
    d  Fettstoffe

643 FEED CONSUMPTION
    f  Consommation de fourrage
    d  Futterverbrauch

644 FERMENTATION INDUSTRY
    f  Industrie des boissons
       fermentées
    d  Gärungsindustrie

645 FERTILIZATION
    f  Fumure
    d  Düngung

646 FERTILIZER FACTORY
    f  Usine d'engrais
    d  Düngerfabrik

647 FERTILIZER INDUSTRY
    f  Industrie des engrais
    d  Düngemittelindustrie

648 FERTILIZER TRIALS
    f  Essai de fertilisation
    d  Düngungstest

649 CHEMICAL FERTILIZER
    f  Engrais chimique
    d  Chemischer Dünger

650 ORGANIC FERTILIZER
    f  Engrais organique
    d  Organischer Dünger

651 USE OF FERTILIZER
    f  Emploi des engrais
    d  Verwendung von Dünge-
       mitteln

652 FISH BREEDING;
    FISH FARMING
    f  Pisciculture
    d  Fischzucht

653 SPECIES OF FISH
    f  Espèces de poissons
    d  Fischarten

654 FISHERIES
   f  Industrie de pêche
   d  Fischfang

655 FISHERIES DEVELOPMENT
   f  Développement des pêches
   d  Fischereientwicklung

656 FISHING EQUIPMENT
   f  Attirail de pêche
   d  Fischfangausrüstung

657 FISHING FLEET
   f  Armement à la pêche
   d  Fischflotte

658 FISHING METHODS
   f  Systèmes de pêche
   d  Fischfangmethoden

659 COASTAL FISHING
   f  Pêche littorale
   d  Küstenfischfang

660 OCEAN FISHING
   f  Pêche maritime
   d  Hochseefischerei

661 TRADITIONAL FISHING
   f  Pêche traditionnelle
   d  Traditioneller Fischfang

662 TUNNY FISHING
   f  Pêche thonière
   d  Thunfischfang

663 TUNNY FISHING BOAT
   f  Navire thonier
   d  Thunfischfänger

664 TECHNIQUES OF FISHING
   f  Techniques de la pêche
   d  Fangtechnik

665 FLORICULTURE
   f  Floriculture
   d  Blumenkultur

666 FOOD;
FOODSTUFFS
   f  Aliments;

     Denrées alimentaires
   d  Nahrungsmittel;
     Lebensmittel

667 FOOD AID
   f  Aide alimentaire
   d  Nahrungsmittelhilfe

668 FOOD CONSUMPTION
   f  Consommation alimentaire
   d  Nahrungskonsum

669 FOOD CROPS
   f  Cultures vivrières
   d  Nahrungsmittelkulturen

670 FOOD ECONOMY
   f  Alimentation
   d  Ernährungswirtschaft

671 FOOD INDUSTRY
   f  Industrie alimentaire
   d  Nahrungsmittelindustrie

672 FOOD NUTRITION
   f  Alimentation;
     Nutrition
   d  Ernährung

673 FOOD PROCESSING
   f  Transformation de produits
     alimentaires
   d  Nahrungsmittelverarbei-
     tung

674 FOOD PRODUCTION
   f  Production vivrière
   d  Nahrungsmittelproduktion

675 FOOD REQUIREMENTS;
FOOD NEEDS
   f  Besoins alimentaires
   d  Nahrungsmittelbedarf

676 FOOD SUPPLIES
   f  Approvisionnement en
     aliments
   d  Nahrungsmittel-
     beschaffung

699 IMPROVEMENT OF
AGRICULTURE
f Amélioration de
l'agriculture
d Verbesserung der
Landwirtschaft

700 IRRIGATION
INSTALLATIONS
f Installations d'irrigation
d Bewässerungseinrich-
tungen

701 IRRIGATION ECONOMICS
f Economie de l'irrigation
d Bewässerungswirtschaft

702 IRRIGATION EXTENSION
f Vulgarisation des mé-
thodes d'irrigation
d Bewässerungsvulgarisa-
tion

703 IRRIGATION PROJECTS
f Projets d'irrigation
d Bewässerungsprojekte

704 YEAR-ROUND IRRIGATION;
CONTINUOUS IRRIGATION;
PERMANENT IRRIGATION
f Irrigation sur toute
l'année
d Konstante Bewässerung

705 SEASONAL IRRIGATION
f Irrigation saisonnière
d Saisonale Bewässerung

706 UPLAND IRRIGATION
f Irrigation en montagne
d Berglandbewässerung

707 SYSTEM OF IRRIGATION
f Système d'irrigation
d Bewässerungssystem

708 KOLANUT
f Noix de cola
d Kolanuss

709 LAND APPROPRIATION
f Appropriation de la
terre
d Landaneignung

710 LAND ASSETS
f Capital foncier
d Landreichtum

711 LAND CLEARING
f Défrichage
d Rodung

712 LAND IMPROVEMENT
f Aménagement foncier
d Bodenverbesserung

713 LAND OWNERSHIP
f Propriété foncière
d Landbesitz

714 LAND RECLAMATION
f Défrichement
d Landgewinnung

715 LAND REFORM
f Réforme agraire
d Landreform

716 LAND SYSTEM
f Système agraire
d Agrarsystem

717 LAND TENURE
f Régime foncier
d Landbesitzsystem

718 LAND USE
f Utilisation des terres;
Utilisation du terrain;
Utilisation de la terre
d Landnutzung

719 ARABLE LAND
f Terres arables
d Bebaubares Land

720 CULTIVATED LAND
f Terres sous cultivation;
Périmètre aménagé
d Bebautes Land

721 IRRIGATED LAND
  f Terres irriguées;
    Terrain irrigué
  d Bewässertes Land

722 UNDEVELOPED LAND;
    VIRGIN LAND
  f Terres en friche
  d Ungerodetes Land

723 LARGE LANDHOLDING
  f Grande propriété
    foncière
  d Grossgrundbesitz

724 LAW OF DIMINISHING
    RETURNS
  f Loi du rendement décrois-
    sant du sol
  d Gesetz des abnehmenden
    Bodenertrages

725 LIVE STOCK
  f Bétail
  d Viehbestand;
    Tierbestand

726 LUMBER;
    TIMBER
  f Bois
  d Holz

727 LUMBER INDUSTRY
  f Industrie du bois
  d Holzindustrie

728 MAIZE;
    CORN
  f Maïs
  d Mais

729 MANGOES
  f Mangoes
  d Mangofrüchte

730 MANIOC
  f Manioc
  d Maniok

731 MARKETING OF AGRI-
    CULTURAL PRODUCE
  f Commercialisation des
    produits agricoles
  d Kommerzialisierung
    landwirtschaftlicher
    Produkte;
    Vermarktung

732 MEAT PROCESSING
  f Transformation de la
    viande
  d Fleischverarbeitung

733 COOKED MEAT INDUSTRY
  f Charcuterie industrielle
  d Fleischverarbeitungs-
    industrie;
    Fleischverarbeitende
    Industrie

734 MECHANIZATION OF FARMS;
    FARM MECHANIZATION
  f Mécanisation des entre-
    prises agricoles
  d Mechanisierung von
    landwirtschaftlichen
    Unternehmen

735 MELONS
  f Melons
  d Melonen

736 MILK AND DAIRY PRODUCTS
  f Lait et produits laitiers
  d Milch und Molkerei-
    produkte

737 MILLET
  f Mil
  d Hirse

738 MINERALS
  f Minerais
  d Erze

739 MOLASSE
  f Mélasse
  d Melasse

740 STATE OF NUTRITION
    f  Situation alimentaire
    d  Ernährungslage

741 OILS
    f  Huiles
    d  Öle

742 TUNG OIL;
    CHINA-WOOD OIL
    f  Huile de tung;
       Huile de bois de chine
    d  Holzöl;
       Tungöl

743 OWNER OCCUPANCY;
    SELF-MANAGEMENT
    f  Faire-valoir direct
    d  Eigenbewirtschaftung

744 LARGE LAND OWNER;
    LARGE LAND HOLDER
    f  Grand propriétaire
    d  Grossgrundbesitzer

745 PADDY RICE
    f  Riz paddy
    d  Paddy

746 PALM KERNELS
    f  Amandes palmistes
    d  Palmkerne

747 PALM OIL
    f  Huile de palme
    d  Palmöl

748 PALM OIL CULTIVATION
    f  Culture du palmier à
       huile
    d  Palmölkultur

749 PALM PRODUCE
    f  Produits palmiers
    d  Palmprodukte

750 PASTORAL ECONOMY
    f  Economie pastorale
    d  Weidewirtschaft

751 PATCHULI
    f  Patchouli
    d  Patschuli

752 PERSIAN LAMB
    f  Karakuls
    d  Karakulfelle;
       Persianerfelle

753 PESTS
    f  Parasites;
       Animaux nuisibles
    d  Parasiten

754 PEST CONTROL;
    INSECT CONTROL
    f  Lutte contre les parasites
       des cultures;
       Lutte contre les ennemis
       des cultures
    d  Parasitenkontrolle;
       Schädlingsbekämpfung

755 PHYSICAL CONDITIONS
    f  Conditions physiques
    d  Physische Bedingungen

756 PIASAVA;
    PIASABA
    f  Piassava;
       Pissave
    d  Piassavefasern

757 PINEAPPLE
    f  Ananas
    d  Ananas

758 PISCICULTURE
    f  Economie piscicole
    d  Fischwirtschaft

759 PLANT DISEASES
    f  Maladies des plantes
    d  Pflanzenkrankheiten

760 PLANT SOCIOLOGY
    f  Phytosociologie
    d  Pflanzensoziologie;
       Vegetationskunde

42

761 AROMATIC PLANTS
   f  Plantes aromatiques
   d  Duftstoffpflanzen

762 DYE PLANTS
   f  Plantes tinctoriales
   d  Farbpflanzen

763 FIBRE PLANTS
   f  Plantes à fibres
   d  Faserpflanzen

764 MEDICINAL PLANTS
   f  Plantes médicinales
   d  Arzneipflanzen

765 OIL PLANTS
   f  Plantes oléagineuses
   d  Ölpflanzen

766 PERFUME PLANTS
   f  Plantes à parfum
   d  Parfümpflanzen

767 SPICE PLANTS
   f  Plantes condimentaires
   d  Gewürzpflanzen

768 STIMULANT AND PSEUDO-ALIMENTARY PLANTS
   f  Plantes stimulantes et pseudo-alimentaires
   d  Genussmittelpflanzen

769 TANNING PLANTS
   f  Plantes tannantes
   d  Gerbstoffpflanzen

770 PLANTATIONS
   f  Plantations
   d  Pflanzungen

771 SWEET POTATO
   f  Patate douce
   d  Batate; Süsskartoffel

772 PROCESSING OF FRUITS
   f  Transformation des fruits
   d  Obstverarbeitung

773 PROCESSING OF VEGETABLES
   f  Transformation des légumes
   d  Gemüseverarbeitung

774 BASIC AGRICULTURAL PRODUCTS
   f  Produits agricoles de base
   d  Landwirtschaftliche Ausgangsprodukte

775 SEAWEED PRODUCTS
   f  Produits d'algues
   d  Algenprodukte

776 STAPLE PRODUCT
   f  Produit principal
   d  Hauptprodukt

777 PYRETHRUM
   f  Pyrèthre
   d  Bertram

778 RABBIT KEEPING
   f  Cuniculture
   d  Kaninchenzucht

779 RAINFALL
   f  Pluviosité
   d  Regenfall; Niederschlag

780 CYCLE OF RAIN
   f  Cycle de la pluie
   d  Regenzyklus

781 REFORESTATION
   f  Reboisement
   d  Wiederaufforstung

782 REORGANIZATION OF AGRICULTURE
   f  Reconversion de l'agriculture
   d  Umstellung der Landwirtschaft

783 RICE CULTIVATION
   f  Riziculture
   d  Reiskultur

784 RICE SEASON
   f Campagne rizicole
   d Reiskampagne

785 RUBBER
   f Caoutchouc
   d Gummi

786 RURAL ECONOMY
   f Economie rurale
   d Agrarökonomie;
     Landwirtschaft

787 RURAL ECONOMIST
   f Economiste rural
   d Agrarökonom

788 RURAL PLANNING
   f Planification rurale
   d Planung der ländlichen
     Gebiete;
     Agrarplanung;
     "Grüner Plan"

789 RURAL SOCIOLOGY
   f Sociologie rurale
   d Agrarsoziologie

790 RURAL VITALIZATION
   f Vitalisation rurale
   d Belebung der Landwirt-
     schaft

791 SESAME
   f Sésame
   d Sesam

792 SEED FIELDS
   f Champs semenciers
   d Saatfelder;
     Sämereien

793 SEED PRODUCTION
   f Production des semences
   d Saatproduktion

794 SUNFLOWER SEEDS
   f Graines de tournesol
   d Sonnenblumensamen

795 SHEEP BREEDING
   f Elevage des ovins
   d Schafzucht

796 SILVICULTURE HOSTILITY
   f Attitude hostile à la
     sylviculture
   d Waldfeindliche
     Einstellung

797 SISAL
   f Sisal;
     Agave
   d Sisalagave

798 SLAUGHTERHOUSES
   f Abattoirs
   d Schlachthäuser

799 SOIL CONSERVATION
   f Conservation du sol
   d Bodenerhaltung

800 SOIL IMPROVEMENT;
   LAND RENEWAL
   f Aménagement du sol
   d Bodenverbesserung

801 SOIL SCIENCE;
   PEDOLOGY
   f Science du sol;
     Pédologie
   d Bodenkunde;
     Pedologie

802 SOIL SCIENTIST;
   SOIL TECHNICIAN
   f Pédologue
   d Pedologe

803 SOIL SURVEY
   f Etude des sols;
     Enquête pédologique
   d Pedologische Unter-
     suchung

804 CULTIVATION OF SOIL;
   TILLAGE
   f Travaux du sol
   d Bodenbearbeitung

805 SOY BEANS
   f  Soya
   d  Soyabohnen

806 STABILIZATION OF MOUN-
     TAIN FORESTS
   f  Stabilisation des forêts
     de montagne
   d  Stabilisierung von
     Bergwäldern

807 STANDARDIZATION OF
     AGRICULTURAL PRODUCE
   f  Normalisation des pro-
     duits agricoles
   d  Standardisierung der
     Agrarprodukte

808 STARCH INDUSTRY
   f  Industrie de la fécule
   d  Stärkeindustrie

809 STATE PROPERTIES
   f  Propriétés d'Etat
   d  Staatsgüter

810 SUGAR BEETS
   f  Betteraves à sucre
   d  Zuckerrüben

811 SUGAR CANE
   f  Canne à sucre
   d  Zuckerrohr

812 SUGAR CANE PLANTATION
   f  Plantation de canne à
     sucre
   d  Zuckerrohrplantage

813 SUGAR INDUSTRY
   f  Industrie du sucre
   d  Zuckerindustrie

814 SUGAR MILL
   f  Usine de sucre
   d  Zuckerfabrik

815 SUNSHINE
   f  Isolation
   d  Sonnenbestrahlung

816 TEA
   f  Thé
   d  Tee

817 TECHNICAL LEVEL OF
     AGRICULTURE
   f  Niveau technique
     agricole
   d  Technisches Niveau der
     Landwirtschaft

818 TEXTILE FIBRES
   f  Fibres textiles
   d  Textilpflanzen

819 TROPICAL TIMBER
   f  Bois tropicaux
   d  Tropenholz

820 TYPES OF WOOD;
     VARIETIES OF TIMBER
   f  Espèces de bois;
     Variétés de bois
   d  Holzarten

821 TOBACCO PRODUCTION
   f  Production de tabac
   d  Tabakproduktion

822 TRACTOR
   f  Tracteur
   d  Traktor

823 TROPICAL AGRONOMY
   f  Agronomie tropicale
   d  Tropenlandwirtschafts-
     lehre

824 TROPICAL SEAS
   f  Mers tropicales
   d  Tropische Meere

825 TROPICAL SOIL
   f  Sol tropical
   d  Tropischer Boden

826 TYPES OF FOREST
   f  Formes de forêts
   d  Waldformen

827 TYPES OF STEPPE
    f  Formes de steppes
    d  Steppenformen

828 VANILLA
    f  Vanille
    d  Vanille

829 VEGETABLES
    f  Légumes;
       Légumineuses
    d  Gemüse

830 VEGETABLE FIBRES
    f  Fibres végétales
    d  Pflanzenfasern

831 VEGETABLE OIL
    f  Huile végétale
    d  Pflanzenöl;
       Pflanzliches Öl

832 VEGETABLE PRODUCTION
    f  Production des légumes
    d  Gemüseproduktion

833 VEGETABLE PRODUCTION;
    CROP PRODUCTION
    f  Production végétale
    d  Pflanzenproduktion

834 VEGETABLE SILK
    f  Soie végétale
    d  Pflanzenseide

835 EARLY VEGETABLES;
    FRESH VEGETABLES
    f  Primeurs;
       Légumes frais
    d  Frischgemüse

836 VEGETATION
    f  Flore
    d  Flora;
       Vegetation

837 VETERINARY EXPERIMEN-
    TAL STATION
    f  Station vétérinaire
       expérimentale
    d  Veterinärmedizinische
       Versuchsstation

838 VETERINARY SCIENCE
    f  Science vétérinaire
    d  Veterinärwissenschaft

839 VITICULTURE
    f  Viticulture
    d  Weinbau

840 WASTE OF NATURAL
    RESOURCES
    f  Exploitation abusive
    d  Raubbau

841 WATER SUPPLY NETWORK
    f  Réseau de distribution
       d'eau
    d  Wasserversorgungsnetz

842 DRINKING WATER
    f  Eau potable
    d  Trinkwasser

843 UNDERGROUND WATER
    f  Eaux souterraines
    d  Grundwasser

844 WEEDING OPERATIONS
    f  Sarclage
    d  Ausrodung

845 WEEDS
    f  Mauvaises herbes
    d  Unkräuter

846 WELL DRILLER
    f  Spécialiste en forage de
       puits
    d  Brunnenbauexperte

847 WOOL PRODUCTION
    f  Production de la laine
    d  Wollproduktion

848 YAM
    f  Igname
    d  Igname

# IV.

## INDUSTRY
## INDUSTRIE
## INDUSTRIE

849 BUILDING ACTIVITY
    f   Travaux de construction
    d  Bautätigkeit

850 EXTRACTIVE ACTIVITY
    f   Activité extractive
    d  Extraktive Tätigkeit

851 INDUSTRIAL ACTIVITY
    f   Activité industrielle
    d  Industrielle Tätigkeit

852 NON-EXTRACTIVE
    ACTIVITY
    f   Activité non-extractive
    d  Nicht-extraktive
       Tätigkeit

853 TECHNICAL ANALYSIS
    f   Analyse technique
    d  Technische Analyse

854 ASSEMBLY LINE
    f   Travail à la chaîne
    d  Fliessbandarbeit

855 ASSEMBLY WORKSHOP
    f   Atelier de montage
    d  Montagewerkstätte

856 AUTOMOBILE ASSEMBLY
    f   Montage d'automobiles
    d  Montage von Automobilen

857 ATOMIC TECHNIQUES
    f   Techniques atomiques
    d  Atomtechnik

858 BEVERAGES
    f   Boissons
    d  Getränke

859 INDUSTRIAL BOOK-
    KEEPING
    f   Comptabilité industrielle
    d  Industrielle Buchhaltung;
       Industriebuchhaltung

860 BRICK WORKS
    f   Briqueterie
    d  Ziegelei

861 BUILDING FIRM
    f   Firme de construction
    d  Baufirma

862 BOOM IN BUILDING
    f   "Boom" dans la
       construction
    d  "Bauboom"

863 BY-PRODUCT
    f   Sous-produit
    d  Nebenprodukt

864 CANNING
    f   Conservation
    d  Haltbarmachung

865 CAPACITY OF OUTPUT
    f   Capacité de production
    d  Produktionskapazität

866 EXCESS CAPACITY
    f   Capacité excédentaire
    d  Überkapazität

867 OVERALL CAPACITY
    f   Capacité globale
    d  Gesamtkapazität

868 CARD-INDEX OF FIRMS
    f   Fichier des entreprises
    d  Liste von Unternehmen

869 OPEN-CAST
    f   Exploitations minières
       à ciel
    d  Tagbau

870 CEMENT FACTORY
    f   Cimenterie
    d  Zementfabrik

871 CEMENT INDUSTRY
    f   Cimenteries
    d  Zementindustrie

872 TECHNICAL CHANGE
    f   Changement technique
    d  Technischer Wandel

873 CHEMICALS
    f   Produits chimiques
    d  Chemische Produkte

874 CHOICE OF TECHNIQUES
    f   Choix des techniques
    d  Wahl der Technik

875 CLAY
    f   Argile
    d  Ton; Lehm

876 COAL FIELDS
    f   Centres charbonniers
    d  Kohlenfelder

877 COAL RESERVES
    f   Réserves de charbon
    d  Kohlenreserven

878 COAL AND STEEL
    ENTERPRISES
    f   Charbonnages et
       aciéries
    d  Kohle- und Stahl Unter-
       nehmen

879 TECHNICAL COMPLEX
    f   Complexe technique
    d  Technischer Komplex

880 INDUSTRIAL CONCEN-
    TRATION
    f   Concentration industrielle
    d  Industrielle Konzen-
       tration

881 CONCRETE
    f   Béton armé
    d  Zement

882 CONSTRUCTION
    f   Construction
    d  Bauwesen

883 CONSTRUCTION PERIOD
    f   Période de construction
    d  Konstruktionsperiode

884 CONVERSION COSTS
    f   Coûts de transformation
    d  Transformationskosten

885 COPPER
    f   Cuivre
    d  Kupfer

886 COTTON MILL
    f   Filature de coton
    d  Baumwollspinnerei

887 CRAFTS
    f   Artisanat
    d  Handwerk

888 CRAFT ORGANIZATION
    f   Coopérative d'artisans
    d  Handwerksgenossenschaft

889 CRAFT WORKER
    f   Ouvrier artisanal
    d  Handwerker

890 PRODUCTION CRAFT
    f   Artisanat de production
    d  Produktionsgewerbe

891 SERVICE CRAFT
    f   Artisanat de service
    d  Dienstleistungsgewerbe

892 SMALL CRAFTS
    f   Artisanat
    d  Handwerk

893 ARTS AND CRAFTS
    f  Industries d'art
    d  Kunstgewerbe

894 PROMOTION OF CRAFTS
    f  Promotion de l'artisanat
    d  Gewerbeförderung

895 DAM DESIGNER
    f  Spécialiste des études
       de barrages
    d  Experte für Dammbauten

896 HIGH DAM
    f  Barrage
    d  Staudamm

897 DAM CONSTRUCTION
    f  Travaux de construction
       d'un barrage
    d  Stauarbeiten

898 DEPOSIT
    f  Gisement
    d  Lager;
       Vorkommen

899 DERRICK
    f  Derrick
    d  Bohrturm

900 ARTISAN DIAMONDS
    f  Diamants artisanaux
    d  Künstliche Diamanten

901 DISTRIBUTION FACILITIES
FOR ELECTRICITY
    f  Installations de distribu-
       tion de l'électricité
    d  Verteilungseinrichtungen
       für Elektrizität

902 TECHNICAL DOCUMENTA-
TION
    f  Documentation technique
    d  Technische Dokumen-
       tation

903 DRILLING WORK
    f  Forage
    d  Bohrung

904 ELECTRIFICATION
    f  Electrification
    d  Elektrifizierung

905 ELECTRIC POWER STATION;
ELECTRIC POWER PLANT
    f  Centrale électrique
    d  Kraftwerk;
       Elektrizitätswerk

906 HYDRO-ELECTRICITY
    f  Energie hydro-électrique
    d  Wasserkraft

907 ENERGY REQUIREMENTS
    f  Besoins en énergie
    d  Energiebedarf

908 ENERGY RECOURCES
    f  Ressources en énergie
    d  Energiequellen

909 LOCALLY PRODUCED
ENERGY
    f  Energie produite
       localement
    d  Lokale Energie

910 NUCLEAR ENERGY
    f  Energie nucléaire
    d  Nukleare Energie;
       Kernenergie

911 SOLAR ENERGY
    f  Energie solaire
    d  Sonnenenergie

912 ECONOMICS OF ENERGY
    f  Economie de l'énergie
    d  Energiewirtschaft

913 TRADITIONAL SOURCES OF
ENERGY (SUN AND WIND)
    f  Sources d'énergie tradi-
       tionnelles (soleil et vent)
    d  Traditionelle Energie-
       quellen (Sonne und Wind)

914 INDUSTRIAL ENGINEERING
    f  Construction mécanique
    d  Maschinenbau

915 STRUCTURAL ENGINEERING
    f  Technique de la construc-
       tion
    d  Konstruktionstechnik

916 GOVERNMENT ENTERPRISE
    f  Entreprise d'Etat
    d  Staatliches Unternehmen

917 PRIVATE ENTERPRISE
    f  Entreprise privée
    d  Privates Unternehmen

918 EXTRACTION
    f  Exploitation
    d  Abbau;
       Förderung

919 TECHNICAL FACTORS
    f  Facteurs techniques
    d  Technische Faktoren

920 INDUSTRIAL FACTORS
    f  Facteurs industriels
    d  Industrielle Faktoren

921 TECHNICALLY FEASIBLE
    f  Techniquement réalisable
    d  Technisch durchführbar

922 FERTILIZER FACTORY
    f  Fabrique d'engrais
    d  Düngemittelfabrik

923 FINISHED PRODUCT
    f  Produit fini
    d  Endprodukt;
       Fertigprodukt

924 FORMS OF INDUSTRIAL
    ENTERPRISES
    f  Formes d'entreprises
       industrielles
    d  Formen industrieller
       Unternehmen

925 NATURAL GAS
    f  Gaz naturel
    d  Erdgas

926 RESERVES OF NATURAL
    GAS
    f  Réserves de gaz naturel
    d  Erdgasvorkommen

927 GEOLOGICAL RESEARCH
    f  Recherches géologiques
    d  Geologische Forschung

928 GLASS FACTORY
    f  Usine de verre
    d  Glasfabrik

929 GOODS AND SERVICES
    f  Biens et services
    d  Güter und Dienst-
       leistungen

930 HYDROELECTRIC POWER
    f  Energie hydro-électrique
    d  Wasserkraft

931 INDEX OF INDUSTRIAL
    PRODUCTION
    f  Indice de la production
       industrielle
    d  Produktionsindex

932 INDUSTRIAL AGE;
    AGE OF INDUSTRY
    f  Epoque industrielle;
       Age d'industrialisation
    d  Industriezeitalter

933 INDUSTRIAL AGREEMENT
    f  Accord industriel
    d  Industrieabkommen

934 INDUSTRIAL ANALYSIS
    f  Analyse industrielle
    d  Industrielle Analyse

935 INDUSTRIAL CENTRE
    f  Centre industriel
    d  Industriezentrum

936 INDUSTRIAL RESIDENTIAL
    CENTRE
    f  Cité ouvrière
    d  Wohnzentrum für
       Industriearbeiter

937 INDUSTRIAL COMPLEX
  f  Complex industriel
  d  Industriekomplex

938 INDUSTRIAL COOPERATION
  f  Coopération industrielle
  d  Industrielle Kooperation

939 INDUSTRIAL DEVELOP-
    MENT
  f  Développement industriel
  d  Industrieentwicklung

940 INDUSTRIAL ECONOMIST;
    INDUSTRIAL EXPERT
  f  Economiste spécialisé
     dans les matières
     industrielles;
     Economiste industriel
  d  Industrieexperte

941 INDUSTRIAL ECONOMY
  f  Economie industrielle
  d  Industriewirtschaft

942 INDUSTRIAL ENTERPRISE
  f  Entreprise industrielle
  d  Industrieunternehmen

943 INDUSTRIAL EXPANSION
  f  Expansion industrielle
  d  Industrielle Expansion

944 INDUSTRIAL FAIRS
  f  Foires industrielles
  d  Industriemessen

945 INDUSTRIAL GEOGRAPHY
  f  Géographie industrielle
  d  Industriegeographie

946 INDUSTRIAL GROWTH
  f  Croissance industrielle
  d  Industrielles Wachstum

947 INDUSTRIAL INFORMATION
  f  Information industrielle
  d  Information auf dem
     Industriesektor

948 INDUSTRIAL LEADERSHIP
  f  Prépondérance industrielle
  d  Industrielle Führung

949 INDUSTRIAL LEGISLATION
  f  Législation industrielle
  d  Gesetzgebung auf dem
     Industriesektor

950 INDUSTRIES LOCATION;
    INDUSTRIAL LOCATION
  f  Choix de l'emplacement
     des entreprises;
     Localisation industrielle
  d  Lokalisierung von
     Industrieanlagen

951 INDUSTRIAL MACHINERY
  f  Machines industrielles
  d  Industriemaschinen

952 INDUSTRIAL PLANNING
  f  Planification industrielle
  d  Industrieplanung

953 INDUSTRIAL POLICY
  f  Politique industrielle
  d  Industriepolitik

954 INDUSTRIAL PLANT
  f  Ensemble industriel;
     Exploitation industrielle
  d  Industrieanlage;
     Industriebetrieb

955 INDUSTRIAL POTENTIAL
  f  Potentiel industriel
  d  Industriepotential

956 INDUSTRIAL PRODUCT
  f  Produit industriel
  d  Industrieprodukt

957 INDUSTRIAL PRODUCTION
  f  Production industrielle
  d  Industrieproduktion

958 INDUSTRIAL PROMOTION
  f  Promotion industrielle
  d  Industrieförderung

959 INDUSTRIAL PROPERTY
   f  Propriété industrielle
   d  Industrielles Eigentum

960 INDUSTRIAL PSYCHOLOGY
   f  Psychotechnique;
      Psychologie industrielle
   d  Industriepsychologie

961 INDUSTRIAL RESEARCH
   f  Recherches industrielles
   d  Industrieforschung

962 INDUSTRIAL SECTOR
   f  Secteur industriel
   d  Industriesektor

963 INDUSTRIAL SOCIETY
   f  Société industrielle
   d  Industriegesellschaft

964 INDUSTRIAL SOCIOLOGY
   f  Sociologie industrielle
   d  Industriesoziologie

965 INDUSTRIAL STRUCTURE
   f  Structures industrielles
   d  Industriestruktur

966 INDUSTRIAL TRADITION
   f  Tradition industrielle
   d  Industrielle Tradition

967 INDUSTRIAL UNIT
   f  Unité industrielle
   d  Industrieeinheit

968 INDUSTRIAL WATERS
   f  Eaux à usages industriels
   d  Industriegewässer

969 INDUSTRIAL WORKERS
   f  Ouvriers industriels;
      Travailleurs industriels
   d  Industriearbeiter

970 INDUSTRIALIZATION PLAN
   f  Plan d'industrialisation
   d  Industrialisierungsplan

971 INDUSTRIALIZATION
   PROBLEMS
   f  Problèmes d'industriali-
      sation
   d  Industrialisierungspro-
      bleme

972 INDUSTRIALIZATION
   PROJECTS
   f  Projets d'industrialisation
   d  Industrialisierungs-
      projekte

973 ACCELERATED INDUSTRIA-
   LIZATION
   f  Industrialisation
      accélérée
   d  Beschleunigte Industria-
      lisierung

974 COLONIAL INDUSTRIALI-
   ZATION
   f  Industrialisation
      coloniale
   d  Koloniale Industriali-
      sierung

975 DELAY IN INDUSTRIALI-
   ZING
   f  Retards dans l'industria-
      lisation
   d  Verzögerung in der
      Industrialisierung

976 AFRICAN INDUSTRY
   f  Industrie africaine
   d  Afrikanische Industrie

977 ALLIED INDUSTRY
   f  Industrie annexe
   d  Angeschlossene Industrie

978 BASIC INDUSTRY
   f  Industrie de base
   d  Basisindustrie

979 BEVERAGE INDUSTRY
   f  Industrie des boissons
   d  Getränkeindustrie

980 INDUSTRY IN THE
FRONTIER REGIONS;
BORDER INDUSTRY
f Industrie frontalière
d Industrie in den Grenz-
gebieten

981 BREWING INDUSTRY
f Production brassicole
d Bierbrauerei;
Bierindustrie

982 BUILDING INDUSTRY
f Industrie du bâtiment
d Konstruktionsindustrie

983 CANNING INDUSTRY
f Conserverie
d Konservenindustrie

984 CAPITAL GOODS
INDUSTRIES
f Industrie de biens
d'équipement
d Kapitalgüterindustrie

985 CHEMICAL INDUSTRY
f Industrie chimique
d Chemische Industrie

986 CLOTHING INDUSTRY
f Industrie de confection
d Bekleidungsindustrie

987 CONSUMER GOODS
INDUSTRY
f Industrie de biens de
consommation
d Konsumgüterindustrie

988 DEPARTMENT OF INDUSTRY
f Services de l'industrie
d Industrieministerium

989 DERIVED INDUSTRY
f Industrie dérivée
d Abgeleitete Industrie

990 DOMESTIC INDUSTRY;
COTTAGE INDUSTRY
f Industrie à domicile
d Heimindustrie

991 ELECTRICAL INDUSTRY
f Industrie électrique
d Elektrische Industrie

992 FOOD INDUSTRY;
FOOD PROCESSING
INDUSTRY
f Industrie alimentaire
d Nahrungsmittelindustrie

993 FOOTLOOSE INDUSTRY
f Industrie mobile
d Mobile Industrie

994 GROWTH-INDUSTRY
f Industrie de croissance
d Wachstumsindustrie

995 HEAVY INDUSTRY
f Industrie lourde
d Schwerindustrie

996 HOME INDUSTRY
f Industrie nationale
d Einheimische Industrie

997 IRON AND STEEL INDUSTRY
f Industrie du fer et de
l'acier;
Sidérurgie
d Eisen- und Stahlindustrie

998 KEY INDUSTRY;
INSTRUMENTAL INDUSTRY
f Industrie clef
d Schlüsselindustrie

999 LEATHER INDUSTRY
f Industrie du cuir
d Lederindustrie

1000 LIGHT INDUSTRY
f Industrie légère
d Leichtindustrie

1001 LOCAL INDUSTRY;
REGIONAL INDUSTRY
f Industrie locale;
Industrie régionale
d Lokale Industrie

1002 LUXURY GOODS INDUSTRY
    f   Industrie de luxe
    d   Luxusgüterindustrie

1003 MACHINE INDUSTRY
    f   Industrie mécanique
    d   Maschinenindustrie

1004 MANUFACTURING
       INDUSTRY
    f   Industrie manufacturière
    d   Verarbeitende Industrie

1005 MEAT INDUSTRY
    f   Industrie animale
    d   Industrielle Fleischver-
        arbeitung

1006 MECHANICAL INDUSTRY
    f   Industrie mécanique
    d   Mechanische Industrie

1007 MISCELLANEOUS
       INDUSTRIES
    f   Industries diverses
    d   Verschiedene Industrien

1008 MOTOR INDUSTRY
    f   Industrie automobile
    d   Autoindustrie

1009 PACKAGING INDUSTRY
    f   Industrie d'emballage
    d   Verpackungsindustrie

1010 PAPER INDUSTRY
    f   Industrie papetière
    d   Papierindustrie

1011 PARTICULAR INDUSTRY
    f   Industrie particulière
    d   Einzelindustrie

1012 PETROLEUM INDUSTRY;
       OIL INDUSTRY
    f   Industrie de pétrole;
        Industrie pétrolière
    d   Erdölindustrie

1013 PLASTIC INDUSTRY
    f   Industrie de matières
        plastiques
    d   Kunststoffindustrie

1014 PIONEER INDUSTRY
    f   Industrie pilote
    d   Pionierindustrie

1015 PROCESSING INDUSTRY
    f   Industrie de transforma-
        tion
    d   Verarbeitungsindustrie

1016 PROJECTS FOR INDUSTRY
    f   Projets pour l'industrie
    d   Industrieprojekte

1017 REPRESENTATIVE
       INDUSTRY
    f   Industrie type;
        Industrie représentative
    d   Industrietype

1018 REQUIREMENTS OF
       INDUSTRY
    f   Besoins de l'industrie
    d   Industriebedürfnisse

1019 RESIDENTIARY INDUSTRY;
       IMMOBILE INDUSTRY
    f   Industrie située à
        proximité des consomma-
        teurs;
        Industrie immobile
    d   Immobile Industrie

1020 RUBBER INDUSTRY
    f   Industrie de caoutchouc
    d   Gummiindustrie

1021 SMALL-SCALE INDUSTRY
    f   Petite industrie
    d   Kleine Industrie

1022 TEXTILE INDUSTRY
    f   Industrie textile
    d   Textilindustrie

1023 TRANSFORMATION
       INDUSTRY
    f   Industrie de transforma-
        tion
    d   Transformationsindustrie

1024 EXPENDITURE ON
INDUSTRY
f  Dépenses au titre de
l'industrie
d  Industrieausgaben

1025 INSTALLATIONS
f  Installations
d  Anlagen

1026 INSTALLATION
TECHNICIAN
f  Monteur
d  Montagespezialist

1027 COMPLEMENTARY
INSTALLATIONS
f  Installations complémentaires
d  Zusatzeinrichtungen

1028 MOBILE INSTALLATIONS
FOR ASSEMBLING
EQUIPMENT
f  Installations mobiles de
montage
d  Mobile Montageein-
richtungen

1029 HYDROELECTRIC INTER-
CONNECTION SYSTEMS
f  Systèmes d'interconnec-
tion hydro-électriques
d  Hydroelektrische Verbund-
systeme

1030 INTER-INDUSTRIAL
RELATIONSHIP
f  Relations inter-indus-
trielles
d  Interindustrielle
Beziehungen

1031 IRON ORES
f  Minerais de fer
d  Eisenerze

1032 LABORATORY FACILITIES
f  Laboratoires
d  Laboranlagen

1033 LABOUR DIVISION
f  Division du travail
d  Arbeitsteilung

1034 LIMESTONE DEPOSIT
f  Gisement de calcaire
d  Kalkvorkommen

1035 LOCATION THEORY
f  Théorie de l'impantation
d  Lokalisierungstheorie

1036 MACHINE TOOLS
f  Machine-outils
d  Maschinenwerkzeuge

1037 SEMI-AUTOMATIC
MACHINES
f  Machines semi-auto-
matiques
d  Halbautomatische
Maschinen

1038 PER CAPITA CONSUMPTION
OF MACHINERY
f  Machines disponibles
par tête d'habitant
d  Per capita Konsum an
Maschinen

1039 HOTEL MANAGEMENT;
HOTEL BUSINESS
f  Industrie hôtelière
d  Hotelindustrie

1040 INDUSTRIAL MANAGEMENT
f  Organisation des entre-
prises
d  Organisation der Unternehmen

1041 PLANT MANAGEMENT
f  Gestion des installations
d  Verwaltung der
Produktionsstätten

1042 LOCAL MANUFACTURE
f  Manufactures locales
d  Lokale Erzeugung

1043 MANUFACTURING
f Fabrication
d Produktion

1044 MANUFACTURING PROCESS
f Processus de confection
d Verarbeitungsprozess

1045 MATERIAL TESTING
f Essai de matériaux
d Werkstoffprüfung

1046 MASS-PRODUCED GOODS
f Produits de grande série
d Massenprodukte

1047 METAL PRODUCTION
f Production des métaux
d Metallproduktion

1048 METAL WORKS
f Industrie métallurgique;
Métallurgie
d Metallindustrie

1049 SAWMILL
f Travaux de sciage
d Sägewerk

1050 STEEL MILL
f Usine sidérurgique
d Stahlwerk

1051 SPINNING MILL
f Filature
d Spinnerei

1052 SUGAR MILL
f Usine de sucre
d Zuckerfabrik

1053 WEAVING MILL
f Tissage
d Weberei

1054 MINERAL RESOURCES;
MINERAL WEALTH
f Richesses du sous-sol
d Bodenschätze

1055 MINERAL RESOURCES
DEVELOPMENT
f Mise en valeur des
ressources minérales
d Entwicklung minera-
lischer Reserven

1056 MINERALOGY
f Minéralogie
d Mineralogie

1057 MINING COMPANY
f Société minière
d Bergwerksgesellschaft

1058 MINING ECONOMY
f Economie minière
d Bergbauwirtschaft

1059 MINING PRODUCTION
f Production minière
d Bergbauproduktion

1060 MINING RIGHTS
f Titres minières
d Schürfrechte

1061 MINING AND QUARRYING
f Industrie d'extraction
d Extraktionsindustrie

1062 DISTRIBUTION NETWORK
f Réseau de distribution
d Versorgungsnetz

1063 INDUSTRIAL OCCUPATION
CLASSIFICATION
f Population classée par
activité industrielle
d Klassifizierung
industrieller Arbeits-
plätze

1064 OIL AGREEMENT
f Accord pétrolier
d Erdölabkommen

1065 OIL DEPOSITS
f Gisements de pétrole
d Erdölvorkommen

1066 OIL EXPLORATION
f Prospection pétrolière
d Erdölaufsuchung

1067 OIL FIELDS
f Champs pétrolifères
d Ölfelder

1068 CRUDE OIL
f Mazout
d Rohöl

1069 OIL AND BY-PRODUCTS
f Pétrole et dérivés
d Ölprodukte und Derivate

1070 ORGANIZATION OF
INDUSTRIAL ZONES
f Organisation des zones
industrielles
d Organisation von
Industriezonen

1071 OPERATING COSTS
f Coûts d'exploitation
d Gewinnungskosten

1072 TYPE OF OPERATION
f Conditions d'exploitation
d Gewinnungsbedingungen

1073 PAINTS FACTORY
f Usine de peintures
d Farbenfabrik

1074 PATTERN OF INDUSTRIAL
OUTPUT
f Composition de la production industrielle
d Struktur der industriellen
Produktion

1075 CRUDE PETROLEUM
f Pétrole brut
d Rohöl

1076 PIPELINE
f Pipe-line;
Oléoduc
d Pipeline;
Erdölleitung

1077 UNDER WATER PIPE
f Conduite sous-marine
d Unterwasserleitung

1078 PLANT;
FACTORY;
MILL
f Usine
d Fabrik

1079 PILOT PLANT
f Atelier pilote
d Modellanlage;
Mustereinrichtung

1080 POTASH
f Potasse
d Kali

1081 POWER DEVELOPMENT
f Développement de
l'énergie
d Energieentwicklung

1082 POWER PRODUCTION
f Production de l'énergie
d Energieproduktion

1083 ELECTRIC POWER
f Energie électrique
d Elektrische Energie

1084 EXPERT ON POWER
f Expert de l'énergie
d Energieexperte

1085 THERMAL POWER
f Energie thermique
d Thermale Energie

1086 PREFABRICATION
f Construction préfabriquée
d Vorfabrikation

1087 PROCESSED PRODUCT
f Produit transformé
d Veredeltes Produkt;
Veredlungsprodukt

1088 PROCESSING FACTORY
f Usine de traitement
d Anlage zur Verarbeitung

1109 SYNTHETIC FUEL
f   Carburant synthétique
d   Synthetischer Kraftstoff

1110 EXPERIMENTAL TECHNO-
LOGY
f   Technologie expérimen-
tale
d   Experimentelle Technologie

1111 OBSOLESCENT TECHNO-
LOGY
f   Technologie surannée
d   Veraltete Technologie

1112 PETROLEUM TECHNOLOGY
f   Technologie du pétrole
d   Erdöltechnik

1113 TEXTILE FACTORY
f   Usine textile
d   Textilfabrik

1114 TIN
f   Etain
d   Zinn

1115 TOOLS
f   Outils
d   Werkzeuge

1116 TOURISM FOR PLEASURE
f   Tourisme d'agrément
d   Vergnügungstourismus

1117 COMMERCIAL TOURISM
f   Tourisme commercial
d   Kommerzieller Fremden-
verkehr

1118 LUXURY TOURISM
f   Tourisme de grand
standing
d   Luxustourismus

1119 MASS TOURISM
f   Tourisme populaire
d   Massentourismus

1120 TOURIST CENTRE
f   Centre touristique
d   Touristikzentrum

1121 TOURIST INDUSTRY
f   Industrie du tourisme
d   Industrietouristik;
Fremdenverkehrsindustrie

1122 TOURIST LINES
f   Circuits touristiques
d   Touristikströme

1123 DOMESTIC TOURIST TRADE
f   Tourisme intérieur
d   Lokale Touristik

1124 INTERNATIONAL TOURIST
TRADE
f   Tourisme international
d   Internationale Touristik

1125 TOURIST TRAFFIC
f   Industrie du tourisme
d   Touristik

1126 TRIBOLOGY
f   Tribologie
d   Tribologie

1127 FOREIGN UNDERTAKING
f   Entreprise étrangère
d   Ausländisches Unter-
nehmen

1128 WATER RESOURCES
f   Potentiel hydraulique;
Ressources en eaux
d   Wasserreserven

1129 WATER SUPPLY
f   Approvisionnement en
eaux
d   Wasserversorgung

1130 PLANT TO DESALINATE
SEA WATER
f   Usine de traitement
d'eau de mer
d   Anlage zur Entsalzung
des Meerwassers

60

1131 UNDERGROUND WATER
UTILIZATION
f Utilisation des eaux
souterraines
d Grundwasserverwertung

1132 WOOD INDUSTRY
f Industrie du bois
d Holzindustrie

# V.

## TRANSPORT AND COMMUNICATION
## TRANSPORT ET COMMUNICATION
## TRANSPORT UND KOMMUNIKATION

1133 AIR LINE COMPANY
    f  Compagnie aérienne
    d  Fluggesellschaft

1134 AIR ROUTE
    f  Ligne aérienne
    d  Fluglinie;
       Flugstrecke;
       Flugroute

1135 AIR TAXI
    f  Avion taxi
    d  Lufttaxi

1136 AIRCRAFT INDUSTRY
    f  Industrie aéronautique
    d  Flugzeugindustrie

1137 ALLOCATION OF TRAFFIC
    f  Répartition du trafic
    d  Verteilung des Transport-
       netzes;
       Verkehrverteilung

1138 ASPHALT;
    BLACK TOPPING
    f  Asphalt;
       Revêtement bitumé
    d  Asphaltdecke

1139 AUTOPARK
    f  Parc d'automobiles
    d  Autopark

1140 AVIATION
    f  Aviation
    d  Flugwesen

1141 COMMERCIAL AVIATION
    f  Aviation commerciale
    d  Verkehrsfliegerei

1142 BICYCLE PATH
    f  Chemin praticable aux
       bicyclettes
    d  Radweg

1143 TUG BOAT
    f  Remorqueur
    d  Schlepper

1144 CANALS
    f  Canaux
    d  Kanäle

1145 CARGO AIRCRAFT
    f  Avion-cargo
    d  Transportflugzeug

1146 CARGO-HANDLING
    FACILITIES
    f  Installations de
       manutention
    d  Einrichtungen zur
       Manipulation der
       Transportgüter

1147 CARGO STEAMER
    f  Navire cargo
    d  Frachtschiff

1148 AIR CARGO;
    AIR FREIGHT
    f  Frêt aérien
    d  Luftfracht

1149 COASTAL COUNTRY
    f  Pays côtier
    d  Küstenland

1150 CONVEYANCE OF GOODS
    f  Transport de marchandises
    d  Güterbeförderung

1151 CONVEYANCE OF
PASSENGERS
f  Transport de passagers
d  Personenbeförderung

1152 CONVEYER
f  Transporteur;
Convoyeur
d  Frachtführer

1153 CONVEYING DEVICES
f  Installations de transports
d  Fördermittel

1154 GENERAL PURPOSE
CONVEYOR
f  Transporteur universel
d  Allesförderer

1155 CROSS COST
f  Coût total
d  Bruttokosten

1156 FACILITY COST
f  Coût des installations
d  Installationskosten

1157 INITIAL COST
f  Coût initial
d  Anfangskosten

1158 LINE-HAUL COST
f  Coût du parcours de la
ligne
d  Instandhaltungskosten der
Strecke

1159 OPERATING COSTS
f  Dépenses de fonctionne-
ment
d  Betriebskosten

1160 PACKING COST
f  Frais d'emballage
d  Verpackungskosten

1161 RAIL COST
f  Dépenses ferroviaires
d  Schienenstrangkosten

1162 TERMINAL COST
f  Coûts terminaux
d  Endkosten

1163 TRANSPORTATION COST
f  Coût des transports
d  Transportkosten

1164 UNIT COST
f  Coût unitaire
d  Einheitskosten

1165 EXTENSION OF THE
DOCKS
f  Agrandissement des
docks
d  Dockausbau

1166 EARTH WORK OPERATION
f  Opération de terrasse-
ment
d  Trassierungsarbeiten

1167 FERRIES
f  Bacs
d  Fähren

1168 FLIGHT STRIPS
f  Pistes aériennes
d  Luftlinien

1169 FREIGHT
f  Frêt
d  Fracht

1170 FREIGHT BUSINESS;
TRANSPORTATION AGENCY
f  Agence de transport
d  Speditionsgeschäft

1171 FREIGHT TRANSPORTATION
f  Transport de frêt
d  Gütertransport

1172 MARITIME FREIGHT
RATES
f  Taux du frêt maritime
d  Schiffahrtsfrachtraten;
Seefrachtraten

1173 OCEAN FREIGHT
 f Frêt maritime
 d Seefracht

1174 PHANTOM FREIGHT
 f Frêt phantome
 d Überhöhte Transportkosten

1175 RAIL FREIGHT TRAFFIC
 f Transport par voie ferrée
 d Eisenbahngüterverkehr

1176 FUEL CONSUMPTION
 f Consommation de carbu-
 rant
 d Betriebsstoffkonsum

1177 UNIFORM GAUGE IN RAIL-
 WAY SYSTEMS
 f Ecartement entre rail
 standardisé
 d Einheitliche Spurweite

1178 GEOGRAPHIC EQUALI-
 ZATION
 f Egalisation géographique
 d Geographische Nivellie-
 rung

1179 HARBOUR AND PORT
 FACILITIES
 f Ports et installations
 portuaires
 d Hafen und Hafenanlagen

1180 HARBOUR INSTALLATIONS
 f Installations portuaires
 d Hafenanlagen

1181 HARBOUR SPECIALIST
 f Spécialiste en installations portuaires
 d Experte für Hafenanlagen

1182 HARBOUR TRAFFIC
 f Trafic portuaire
 d Hafenverkehr

1183 HIGHWAY BUDGET
 f Budget du réseau routier
 d Strassenbauetat

1184 HIGHWAY CONDITIONS
 f Conditions de la route
 d Strassenbedingungen

1185 HIGHWAY DEVELOPMENT
 TRAINING CENTRE
 f Centre de la formation
 pour le développement du
 réseau routier
 d Ausbildungszentrum zur
 Entwicklung des Strassen-
 netzes

1186 HIGHWAY ENGINEER
 f Ingénieur des Ponts
 et Chaussées
 d Strassenbauingenieur

1187 HIGHWAY FINANCING
 f Financement des routes
 d Finanzierung der Strassen

1188 HIGHWAY ORGANIZATION
 AND MANAGEMENT
 f Organisation et
 administration des routes
 d Organisation und Ver-
 waltung der Strassen

1189 HIGHWAY PLANNING
 f Planification des grandes
 routes
 d Strassenplanung

1190 HIGHWAY SAFETY
 f Sécurité routière
 d Strassensicherheit

1191 HIGHWAY TRANSPORTA-
 TION;
 ROAD TRANSPORTATION
 f Transport routier
 d Strassentransport

1192 MAIN HIGHWAY
 f Route principale
 d Hauptstrasse

1193 PAVED HIGHWAY
 f Route asphaltée;
 Route bitumée
 d Asphaltierte Strasse

1194 STUDIES OF HIGHWAY
NEEDS
f Etudes des besoins en
routes
d Strassenbedarfsstudien

1195 HINTERLAND
f Arrière pays;
Intérieur du pays;
Hinterland
d Hinterland

1196 HITCH
f Attelage
d Anhängevorrichtung

1197 INDUSTRIAL VEHICLE
f Véhicule industriel
d Industriefahrzeug

1198 INFORMATION
f Informations;
Informatique
d Informationswesen

1199 INTEGRATION AXES
f Axes d'intégration
d Integrationsaxen

1200 ISOLATION
f Isolement
d Isolierung

1201 LANDLOCKED COUNTRY
f Pays sans littoral
d Land ohne Zugang zum
Meer

1202 LINES OF PENETRATION
f Lignes de pénétration
d Durchdringungslinien

1203 LOADING AND UNLOADING
f Chargement et décharge-
ment
d Beladen und Entladen

1204 MILEAGE STATISTICS
f Statistiques sur les
kilométrages
d Kilometerstatistik;
Meilenstatistik

1205 INTERNAL AFRICAN
MOVEMENTS
f Mouvements à l'intérieur
de l'Afrique
d Interne afrikanische
Transportbewegungen

1206 TRANSCONTINENTAL
MOVEMENT
f Déplacement transconti-
nental
d Transkontinentale Trans-
portbewegung

1207 RIVER NAVIGATION
f Navigation fluviale
d Binnenschiffahrt

1208 SEA NAVIGATION
f Navigation maritime
d Seetransport

1209 OVERSEAS COUNTRIES
f Pays d'outre-mer
d Überseeländer

1210 PASSENGER CARS
f Voitures de tourisme
d Touristikwagen;
Personenwagen

1211 PORT DUES
f Charges du passage par
le port
d Hafengebühren

1212 PORT INFRASTRUCTURE
f Infrastructure portuaire
d Hafenanlage

1213 PORT INSTALLATIONS
f Installations portuaires
d Hafeneinrichtungen

1214 PORT MANAGEMENT
f Exploitation des ports
d Hafenverwaltung

1215 COMMERCIAL PORT
f Port de commerce
d Handelshafen

1216 FISHING PORT
    f  Port de pêche
    d  Fischerhafen

1217 FREE PORT
    f  Port franc
    d  Freihafen

1218 LOADING AT PORT
    f  Chargement au port
    d  Hafenverladearbeit

1219 POSTAL SERVICE
    f  Service postal
    d  Postdienst

1220 POST TRANSPORTATION
    f  Transport postal
    d  Postbeförderung

1221 RAILROAD NETWORK;
    RAILWAY NETWORK
    f  Réseau ferroviaire
    d  Eisenbahnnetz

1222 RAILROAD TRACK
    f  Voies ferrées
    d  Schienenstrang

1223 RAILROAD TARIFFS
    f  Tarifs ferroviaires
    d  Eisenbahntarife

1224 TRANS-CAMEROON
    RAILWAY
    f  Trans-camerounaise
    d  Transkamerun-Eisenbahn-
       linie

1225 REGULATION OF RATES
    f  Réglementation des tarifs
    d  Tarifbestimmung

1226 UNIT RATE
    f  Tarif unitaire
    d  Einheitstarif

1227 REFRIGERATOR VESSELS
    f  Navires congélateurs
    d  Schiffe mit Kühlanlagen;
       Kühlschiffe

1228 INTERNATIONAL RIVERS
    AND WATERWAYS
    f  Fleuves et canaux
       internationaux
    d  Internationale Flüsse
       und Wasserwege

1229 RISK OF DAMAGE
    f  Risques d'avarie
    d  Beschädigungsrisken

1230 ROAD BUILDING;
    ROAD CONSTRUCTION
    f  Construction des routes
    d  Strassenbau

1231 ROAD "CAPACITY"
    f  "Capacité" routière
    d  "Strassenkapazität"

1232 ROAD DEVELOPMENT
    f  Développement routier
    d  Strassenentwicklung

1233 ROAD LINKS
    f  Liaisons routières
    d  Strassenverbindungen

1234 ROAD MAINTENANCE
    f  Entretien du réseau
       routier
    d  Strasseninstandsetzung

1235 ROAD MAP
    f  Carte routière
    d  Autokarte;
       Strassenkarte;
       Strassenverkehrskarte

1236 ROAD PLANNING
    f  Planification de la
       construction routière
    d  Strassenprojektierung

1237 ROAD POLICY
    f  Politique routière
    d  Strassenpolitik

1238 ROAD SYSTEM
    f  Infrastructure routière;
       Réseau routier
    d  Strassensystem

1239 ROAD USE
    f  Utilisation des routes
    d  Strassenbenützung

1240 ROAD USERS
    f  Utilisateurs des routes
    d  Strassenbenützer

1241 ROAD VEHICLE
    f  Véhicule routier
    d  Strassenfahrzeug

1242 ROAD WORKS
    f  Travaux routiers
    d  Strassenarbeiten

1243 ROADS OF COMMUNICA-
     TIONS
    f  Voies de communications
    d  Verkehrswege

1244 ACCESS ROAD;
     ACCOMODATION ROAD
    f  Route d'accès;
      Route transversale
    d  Zufahrtsstrasse

1245 ALL WEATHER ROAD
    f  Route praticable par tous
      les temps
    d  Allwetterstrasse

1246 BY-ROAD
    f  Route latérale
    d  Nebenstrasse

1247 CROSS-ROAD
    f  Route transversale
    d  Kreuzungsstrasse

1248 DIRT ROAD; DIRT TRACK
    f  Chemin de terre
    d  Trampelpfad; Saumpfad

1249 EARTH ROAD
    f  Piste
    d  Piste; Karrenweg

1250 FEEDER ROADS
    f  Voies de desserte;

      Routes affluentes;
      Routes de collecte
    d  Zubringerstrassen;
      Zufahrtsstrassen

1251 MAIN ROAD
    f  Grande route
    d  Fahrstrasse

1252 ROAD TRANSPORTATION
    f  Transports terrestres
    d  Landverkehr

1253 TWO-LANE ROAD
    f  Route à deux voies
    d  Zweispurige Strasse

1254 CONSTRUCTION OF ROADS
    f  Construction routière
    d  Strassenbau

1255 FARM-TO-MARKET ROADS
    f  Voies entre les zones
      rurales et les marchés
    d  Marktzufahrtswege

1256 LIFE OF THE ROAD
    f  Durée de vie des routes
    d  Lebensdauer einer
      Strasse

1257 PHYSICAL INVENTORY
     OF ROADS
    f  Evaluation des conditions
      physiques des routes
    d  Evaluierung der
      physischen Strassen-
      bedingungen

1258 ROLLING STOCK
    f  Matériel roulant
    d  Rollendes Material

1259 TRANS-SAHARAN ROUTE
    f  Voie trans-saharienne
    d  Transsaharische Strasse

1260 RUNNING SPEED
    f  Vitesse
    d  Geschwindigkeit

1261 RUNWAY
    f  Piste
    d  Piste; Landebahn

1262 SERVICING FACILITIES
    f  Service d'entretien
    d  Instandhaltungsein-
       richtungen

1263 SHIPPING
    f  Navigation
    d  Schiffahrt

1264 SHIPPING PAPERS
    f  Documents d'embarque-
       ment
    d  Schiffspapiere;
       Verladepapiere

1265 SHORTAGE OF MODERN
     EQUIPMENT
    f  Manque d'équipement
       moderne
    d  Mangel an moderner
       Ausstattung

1266 STOCKING DEPOSIT
    f  Parc de stockage;
       Bâtiment de stockage;
       Dépôt
    d  Lagerdepot

1267 STORAGE
    f  Entrepôt de stockage
    d  Lagerareal

1268 STORAGE FACILITIES
    f  Moyens de stockage
    d  Lagerraum

1269 STORAGE UNITS
    f  Unités de stockage
    d  Lagereinrichtungen

1270 STORAGE PERIOD
    f  Période de stockage
    d  Lagerperiode

1271 STREET CODE
    f  Code de la route;
       Règlement de la circula-
       tion
    d  Fahrvorschrift

1272 SURFACE TYPE
    f  Revêtement des routes
    d  Strassenoberfläche

1273 TELECOMMUNICATIONS
    f  Télécommunication
    d  Telekommunikation;
       Nachrichtenverkehr

1274 SPACE TELECOMMUNI-
     CATIONS
    f  Télécommunication
       spatiale
    d  Raumtelekommunikation

1275 TON-KILOMETER
    f  Tonne-kilomètre
    d  Kilometertonne

1276 LARGE TONNAGE
    f  Tonnage important
    d  Grosse Tonnage

1277 TOPOGRAPHY
    f  Topographie
    d  Topographie

1278 TRAFFIC AGREEMENT
    f  Convention de transport
    d  Verkehrsabkommen

1279 TRAFFIC NEEDS;
     TRAFFIC REQUIREMENTS
    f  Besoins du trafic
    d  Verkehrsbedarf

1280 TRAFFIC VOLUME
    f  Densité de la circulation
    d  Verkehrsdichte

1281 AIR TRAFFIC
    f  Trafic aérien
    d  Luftverkehr;
       Flugverkehr

1282 CANAL TRAFFIC
    f  Canal de navigation
    d  Kanalverkehr

1283 COASTAL TRAFFIC
    f  Trafic côtier;
       Cabotage
    d  Küstenverkehr

1284  DOMESTIC TRAFFIC;
      INLAND TRAFFIC
      f  Trafic intérieur
      d  Binnenverkehr

1285  FRONTIER TRAFFIC
      f  Trafic frontalier
      d  Grenzverkehr

1286  LOCAL TRAFFIC
      f  Trafic local
      d  Nahortverkehr

1287  LONG-DISTANCE TRAFFIC
      f  Trafic interurban
      d  Fernverkehr;
         Überlandverkehr

1288  MERCHANDISE TRAFFIC
      f  Trafic commercial
      d  Güterverkehr

1289  PASSENGER TRAFFIC
      f  Trafic des passagers
      d  Passagierverkehr

1290  RAILWAY TRAFFIC;
      RAILROAD TRAFFIC
      f  Transport par chemin de
         fer
      d  Eisenbahnverkehr

1291  ROAD TRAFFIC
      f  Trafic routier
      d  Strassenverkehr

1292  SUBURBAN TRAFFIC
      f  Trafic suburbain
      d  Suburbaner Verkehr

1293  TRANSIT TRAFFIC
      f  Trafic en transit
      d  Transitverkehr

1294  DEVELOPMENT OF
      TRAFFIC
      f  Développement du trafic
      d  Verkehrsentwicklung

1295  PATTERN OF TRAFFIC
      FLOWS
      f  Flux de trafic

      d  Struktur des Verkehrs-
         stromes

1296  TRAILER
      f  Remorque
      d  Anhänger

1297  PERSONS IN TRANSIT
      f  Personnes en transit
      d  Transitpersonen

1298  TRANSPORT EQUIPMENT
      f  Equipement de transports
      d  Transportmittel

1299  TRANSPORT INDUSTRY
      f  Industrie de transports
      d  Transportindustrie

1300  TRANSPORT ECONOMY
      f  Economie de transports
      d  Transportwirtschaft

1301  TRANSPORT SYSTEM
      f  Système des transports
      d  Verkehrssystem

1302  INLAND TRANSPORT
      f  Transports intérieurs
      d  Binnenverkehr

1303  INTERNATIONAL
      TRANSPORTS
      f  Transports internationaux
      d  Internationales Verkehrs-
         wesen

1304  TRANSPORTATION
      SERVICES
      f  Services de transports
      d  Beförderungsleistungen

1305  TRANSPORTATION
      ACCOUNTING
      f  Comptabilité de
         transports
      d  Speditionsbuchführung

1306  TRANSPORTATION
      CHARGES
      f  Frais de transport
      d  Transportkosten

1307 TRANSPORTATION
COMPANY;
FORWARDING AGENCY
f Compagnie de transports
d Verkehrsgesellschaft;
Speditionsgesellschaft

1308 TRANSPORTATION
COORDINATION
f Coordination de trans-
ports
d Transportkoordination

1309 TRANSPORTATION ECONO-
MY
f Economie des transports
d Verkehrswirtschaft

1310 TRANSPORTATION
EQUIPMENT
f Matériel de transports
d Transportmaterial

1311 TRANSPORTATION
FACILITIES
f Facilités de transports
d Verkehrseinrichtungen

1312 TRANSPORTATION EXPERT
f Expert en transports
d Transportsachverständiger;
Transportexperte

1313 TRANSPORTATION INFRA-
STRUCTURE
f Infrastructure du
transport
d Transportinfrastruktur

1314 TRANSPORTATION INDEX
f Indice du transport
d Transportindex

1315 TRANSPORTATION INSU-
RANCE
f Assurance de transports
d Transportversicherung

1316 TRANSPORTATION NET-
WORK
f Réseau du transport
d Transportnetz

1317 TRANSPORTATION
PLANNING
f Planification du
transport
d Transportplanung

1318 TRANSPORTATION PLANS
f Plans de transports
d Transportpläne

1319 TRANSPORTATION POLICY
f Politique de transports
d Transportpolitik

1320 TRANSPORTATION RATE
f Tarif de transports;
Taux de frèt
d Frachttarif;
Transportsätze

1321 TRANSPORTATION ROUTES
f Voies de transports
d Transportwege

1322 TRANSPORTATION
SERVICE
f Service de transports
d Transportwesen

1323 TRANSPORTATION
SURVEY
f Etude sur le transport
d Transportstudie

1324 TRANSPORTATION UNIT
f Unité de transport
d Verkehrsleistung

1325 TRANSPORTATION USERS
f Usagers des moyens de
transport
d Transportbenützer

1326 TRANSPORTATION BY
HELICOPTER
f Transport par hélicoptère
d Helikoptertransport

1327 TRANSPORTATION OF
PASSENGERS
f Transport de passagers
d Personentransport

1328    TRANSPORTATION OF
GOODS
f   Transport de marchandise
d   Frachttransport

1329    AIR TRANSPORTATION
f   Transport aérien
d   Lufttransport

1330    TRANSPORTATION BY AIR;
AIRCRAFT TRANSPORTA-
TION
f   Transport par avion;
Transport aérien
d   Luftfrachtverkehr;
Luftpostbeförderung

1331    INLAND TRANSPORTATION
SYSTEM
f   Système de transport
intérieur
d   Binnentransportsystem

1332    LAND TRANSPORTATION
f   Transports terrestres
d   Landtransport

1333    MARITIME TRANSPORTA-
TION
f   Transports maritimes
d   Schiffstransport

1334    RAPID TRANSPORTATION
f   Transports rapides
d   Schnelltransport

1335    RIVER TRANSPORTATION
f   Transports fluviaux
d   Flusstransport

1336    SEA TRANSPORTATION
f   Transports par mer;
Transports maritimes
d   Seeverfrachtung

1337    FORM OF TRANSPORTATION;
MODE OF TRANSPORTATION
f   Moyens de transports
d   Transportformen

1338    FOREIGN AID FOR
TRANSPORTATION
f   Aide extérieure pour le
développement de
transports
d   Auslandshilfe für
Transportentwicklung

1339    INTEGRATED TRANSPOR-
TATION SYSTEM
f   Système de transport
intégré
d   Integriertes Transport-
system

1340    VOLUME OF TRANSPOR-
TATION
f   Volume de transports
d   Transportvolumen

1341    PROBLEMS OF TRANSPOR-
TATION
f   Problèmes de transports
d   Transportprobleme

1342    TRUCKS
f   Camions
d   Lastwagen

1343    TRUNK LINE HIGHWAYS
f   Axes de concentration
d   Schwerpunktachse

1344    CROSS-COUNTRY VEHICLE
f   Véhicule tous terrains
d   Geländewagen

1345    FARM VEHICLE
f   Véhicule de ferme
d   Landwirtschaftliches
Fahrzeug

1346    WADIS
f   Oueds
d   Wadis

1347    CORN WAGGON;
CORN CART
f   Chariot de moisson
d   Erntewagen

1348   WATERWAYS
    f   Réseau fluvial
    d   Wasserwege

1349   INLAND WATERWAY
    f   Transport fluvial
    d   Nationale Wasserstrasse

1350   EXPRESS WAY;
      FREE WAY
    f   Autoroute
    d   Hauptverkehrsstrasse

# VI.
## INVESTMENTS AND FINANCING
## INVESTISSEMENTS ET FINANCEMENT
## INVESTITIONEN UND FINANZIERUNG

1351 ABSORPTION CAPACITY
    f  Capacité d'absorption
    d  Absorptionsfähigkeit

1352 AMORTIZATION
    f  Amortissement
    d  Abschreibung;
      Amortisation

1353 DOLLAR AREA;
    DOLLAR BLOCK;
    DOLLAR ZONE
    f  Zone dollar
    d  Dollarblock

1354 FRENCH FRANC AREA
    f  Zone franc
    d  Franc-Zone

1355 OVERSEAS STERLING AREA
    f  Zone sterling d'Outre-Mer
    d  Äussere Sterlingzone

1356 ASSETS
    f  Avoirs;
      Actifs
    d  Aktiva

1357 FOREIGN ASSETS
    f  Avoirs extérieurs
    d  Auslandsguthaben

1358 BAZAAR CAPITALISM
    f  Capitalisme de bazar
    d  Basarkapitalismus

1359 BORROWING ARRANGE-
    MENTS
    f  Conventions de crédit
    d  Kreditabkommen

1360 CAPITAL ACCOUNT
    f  Compte de capital
    d  Kapitalkonto

1361 CAPITAL ASSETS
    f  Biens de capital
    d  Kapitalgüter

1362 CAPITAL EQUIPMENT;
    CAPITAL GOODS
    f  Biens d'équipment
    d  Kapitalgüter

1363 CAPITAL EXPENDITURES
    f  Dépenses en capital
    d  Kapitalausgaben

1364 CAPITAL EXPORT
    f  Exportation de capitaux
    d  Kapitalexport

1365 CAPITAL FLIGHT
    f  Exode des capitaux
    d  Kapitalflucht

1366 CAPITAL LOSSES
    f  Pertes en capital
    d  Kapitalverluste

1367 CAPITAL MARKET
    f  Marché des capitaux
    d  Kapitalmarkt

1368 CAPITAL MOVEMENT
    f  Mouvement des capitaux
    d  Kapitalverkehr

1369 CAPITAL RECOVERY
    FACTOR (C.R.F.)
    f  Coefficient d'amortisse-
      ment
    d  Amortisationsfaktor

1370 CAPITAL REQUIREMENTS
  f  Besoins en capitaux
  d  Kapitalbedarf

1371 CAPITAL SHARES
  f  Participation financière
  d  Kapitalanteile

1372 CAPITAL STRUCTURE
  f  Structure de capital
  d  Kapitalstruktur

1373 CAPITAL TRANSACTION
  f  Opération en capital
  d  Kapitaloperation

1374 GROSS FIXED CAPITAL
     FORMATION
  f  Formation brute de
     capital fixe
  d  Bruttofixkapitalbildung

1375 INDUSTRIAL CAPITAL
  f  Capital industriel
  d  Industriekapital

1376 INVESTMENT CAPITAL
  f  Capital d'investissement
  d  Investitionskapital

1377 NEGATIVE CAPITAL
     FORMATION
  f  Formation de capital
     négatif
  d  Kapitalschuld

1378 PRIVATE CAPITAL
  f  Capital privé
  d  Privatkapital

1379 SOCIAL CAPITAL
  f  Capital social
  d  Gesellschaftskapital

1380 WORKING CAPITAL
  f  Fonds de roulement;
     Fonds de fonctionnement
  d  Arbeitskapital

1381 CAPITAL PROTECTIVE
     AGREEMENT
  f  Accord de protection
     des capitaux
  d  Kapitalschutzabkommen

1382 CAPITAL TIED UP IN
     INVENTORY
  f  Capital investi en
     stocks
  d  In der Lagerhaltung
     gebundenes Kapital

1383 INCREMENTAL CAPITAL
     OUTPUT RATIO (ICOR)
  f  Coefficient marginal
     de capital
  d  Kapitalkoeffizient

1384 PARTNERSHIP IN CAPITAL
     PARTICIPATION
  f  Association financière
  d  Kapitalbeteiligung

1385 PROCUREMENT OF
     CAPITAL
  f  Procuration de capitaux
  d  Kapitalbeschaffung

1386 SHORTAGE OF CAPITAL
  f  Manque de capitaux;
     Pénurie de capitaux
  d  Kapitalmangel

1387 IN CASH
  f  En espèces
  d  Barzahlung

1388 INTERNATIONAL CLEARING
     SYSTEM
  f  Clearing international
  d  Internationaler Zahlungs-
     verkehr

1389 DEVELOPMENT
     CONSORTIUM
  f  Consortium de développe-
     ment
  d  Entwicklungskonsortium

1390 COST-BENEFIT RATIO
  f  Rapport coût-bénéfice
  d  Gewinnkoeffizient

1391 ANNUAL COST
    f  Coût annuel
    d  Jährliche Kosten

1392 COMPARATIVE COST
    f  Coût comparé
    d  Komparative Kosten

1393 COMPARATIVE PRODUC-
    TION COSTS
    f  Coûts de production
      comparés
    d  Komparative Produktions-
      kosten

1394 FACTOR COST
    f  Coût des facteurs
    d  Faktorkosten

1395 EXTERNAL COST
    f  Coût externe
    d  Externe Kosten

1396 INITIAL COST
    f  Valeur initiale;
      Coût d'acquisition
    d  Einstandskosten

1397 MARGINAL COST
    f  Coût marginal
    d  Grenzkosten

1398 MONETARY COST
    f  Coût monétaire
    d  Monetäre Kosten

1399 OVERALL COST
    f  Frais globaux
    d  Gesamtkosten

1400 OVERHEAD COST
    f  Frais généraux
    d  Allgemeine Kosten

1401 PROJECT COST
    f  Coût d'un projet
    d  Projektkosten

1402 SOCIAL COST
    f  Coût social
    d  Soziale Kosten

1403 CHANGES IN COST
    f  Variations des coûts
    d  Kostenveränderungen

1404 BORROWING COUNTRY;
    DEBTOR COUNTRY
    f  Pays débiteur
    d  Schuldnerland

1405 CREDITOR COUNTRY;
    LENDING COUNTRY
    f  Pays créditeur
    d  Gläubigerland

1406 DONOR COUNTRY
    f  Pays donateur
    d  Spenderland

1407 EXTENT OF COVERAGE
    f  Taux de couverture
    d  Deckungsausmass;
      Deckungssatz

1408 CREDIT AGREEMENTS
    f  Conventions de crédit
    d  Kreditabkommen

1409 CREDIT COOPERATIVE
    f  Coopérative de crédit
    d  Kreditgenossenschaft

1410 CREDIT ECONOMICS;
    ORGANIZATION OF CREDIT
    f  Organisation du crédit
    d  Kreditorganisation

1411 CREDIT OPERATION;
    CREDIT TRANSACTION
    f  Opération de crédit
    d  Kreditgeschäft

1412 CREDIT POLICY
    f  Politique de crédit
    d  Kreditpolitik

1413 CREDIT RELAXATION;
    EASING OF CREDIT
    f  Facilités de crédit
    d  Krediterleichterung

1414 CREDIT RESERVES
f Crédits non-utilisés
d Kreditreserven

1415 CREDIT RESTRICTION
f Restrictions de crédit
d Kreditbeschränkung

1416 AGRICULTURAL CREDIT;
FARM LOAN
f Crédit agricole
d Agrarkredit

1417 BANK CREDIT
f Crédit bancaire
d Bankkredit

1418 CASH CREDIT
f Crédit de caisse;
Crédit en espèce
d Barkredit

1419 COMMERCIAL CREDIT
f Crédit commercial
d Handelskredit

1420 INDUSTRIAL CREDIT;
LOANS TO INDUSTRY
f Crédit industriel
d Industriekredit

1421 INSTITUTIONAL CREDIT
f Crédit institutionnel
d Institutioneller Kredit

1422 PERSONAL CREDIT;
PERSONAL LOAN
f Crédit personnel
d Persönlicher Kredit

1423 PRIVATE CREDIT
f Crédit privé
d Privater Kredit

1424 PUBLIC CREDIT
f Crédit public
d Öffentlicher Kredit

1425 REAL ESTATE CREDIT
f Crédit immobilier
d Immobilienkredit

1426 SUPERVISED CREDIT
f Crédit contrôlé
d Kontrollierter Kredit

1427 TOTAL CREDIT
f Crédit global
d Globalkredit

1428 CREDIT IN KIND
f Crédit en nature
d Warenkredit

1429 FORMS OF CREDIT
f Formes de crédit
d Kreditformen

1430 GRANTING OF CREDIT
f Octroi de crédit
d Kreditgewährung

1431 DEBT AMORTIZATION;
REPAYMENT OF DEBT
f Amortissement de la dette
d Rückzahlung einer Schuld

1432 DEBT SERVICE
f Service de la dette
d Schuldendienst

1433 DEBTS OF THE DEVELOPING
COUNTRIES
f Endettement des pays en
voie de développement
d Verschuldung der Ent-
wicklungsländer

1434 EXTERNAL DEBT
f Dette extérieure
d Externe Schuld

1435 FOREIGN DEBT
f Dette extérieure
d Auslandsschuld

1436 PERMANENT DEBT
f Dette permanente
d Permanente Schuld

1437 PERPETUAL DEBT
f Dette perpétuelle
d Dauerschuld

1438 PRIVILEGED DEBT
  f  Dette privilégiée
  d  Privilegierte Schuld

1439 PUBLIC DEBT
  f  Dette publique
  d  Öffentliche Schuld

1440 SIGHT DEBT
  f  Dette à vue
  d  Kurzfristige Schuld

1441 TEMPORARY DEBT
  f  Dette temporaire
  d  Temporäre Schuld

1442 DEBTOR ECONOMIC
     SECTOR
  f  Secteur économique
     débiteur
  d  Verschuldeter Wirtschafts-
     sektor

1443 DISECONOMIES
  f  Pertes au coûts
  d  Verluste

1444 DISSAVINGS
  f  Désépargnes;
     Epargne négative
  d  Schulden;
     Passiva

1445 DISTRIBUTION OF PUBLIC
     INVESTMENT
  f  Répartition de l'investisse-
     ment public
  d  Verteilung der öffentlichen
     Investitionen

1446 DOLLAR GAP
  f  Pénurie de dollars
  d  Dollarlücke

1447 DOTATION
  f  Dotation
  d  Dotierung

1448 CAPITAL EXPENDITURES
  f  Dépenses d'équipement
  d  Kapitalausgaben

1449 CURRENT EXPENDITURES
  f  Dépenses de fonctionne-
     ment
  d  Laufende Ausgaben

1450 EXPENDITURES FOR
     DEVELOPMENT PURPOSE
  f  Dépenses de développe-
     ment;
     Dépenses de mise en
     valeur
  d  Ausgaben zu Entwicklungs-
     zwecken

1451 EXPENDITURE ON ESSEN-
     TIAL SERVICES
  f  Investissements d'infra-
     structure
  d  Investitionen für die
     Infrastruktur;
     Infrastrukturinvesti-
     tionen

1452 SECONDARY EXPENSES
  f  Dépenses secondaires
  d  Wirtschaftliche Neben-
     kosten;
     Sekundärausgaben

1453 FINANCIAL DIFFICULTIES
  f  Difficultés financières
  d  Finanzierungsschwierig-
     keiten

1454 FINANCIAL FORECASTING
  f  Prévisions de financement
  d  Finanzierungsplanung

1455 FINANCIAL MANAGEMENT
  f  Organisation financière;
     Direction des finances
  d  Finanzielle Organisation;
     Finanzdirektion

1456 FINANCIAL PARTICIPATION
  f  Participation financière
  d  Finanzierungsbeteiligung

1457 FINANCIAL REQUIREMENTS
  f  Besoins financiers
  d  Finanzielle Bedürfnisse;
     Finanzielle Erfordernisse

1458 FINANCIAL STUDIES
    f  Etudes financières
    d  Finanzierungsstudien

1459 FINANCING METHODS
    f  Méthodes de financement
    d  Finanzierungsmethoden

1460 FINANCING SOURCES
    f  Sources de financement
    d  Finanzierungsquellen

1461 FINANCING OF THE
    ECONOMY
    f  Financement de l'économie
    d  Finanzierung der Wirt-
       schaft

1462 FINANCING OF PLANS
    f  Financement du plan
    d  Finanzierung des Planes

1463 FINANCING THE PURCHASE
    OF CAPITAL GOODS
    f  Financement des achats
       de biens d'équipement
    d  Finanzierung des Ankaufs
       von Kapitalgütern

1464 COMPENSATORY FINANCING
    f  Financement de compen-
       sation
    d  Ausgleichsfinanzierung

1465 DEFICIT FINANCING
    f  Financement par déficit
       budgétaire
    d  Defizitäre Finanzierung

1466 DEVELOPMENT FINANCING
    f  Financement du développe-
       ment
    d  Entwicklungsfinanzierung

1467 DOMESTIC FINANCING
    f  Financement par les
       capitaux intérieurs;
       Financement intérieur
    d  Nationale Finanzierung .

1468 EXTERNAL FINANCING
    f  Financement externe
    d  Externe Finanzierung

1469 METHODS OF FINANCING
    FOREIGN TRADE
    f  Méthodes de financement
       du commerce international
    d  Finanzierungsmethoden
       des Aussenhandels

1470 PREFINANCING
    f  Pré-financement
    d  Vorfinanzierung

1471 SELF-FINANCING
    f  Auto-financement
    d  Eigenfinanzierung

1472 TERMS AND CONDITIONS
    OF FINANCING
    f  Modalités de financement
    d  Finanzierungsarten

1473 FOREIGN CURRENCY
    EARNINGS
    f  Gains de devises
    d  Devisengewinn

1474 SOURCE OF FOREIGN
    CURRENCY
    f  Source de devises
    d  Devisenquelle

1475 FOREIGN EXCHANGE
    EARNINGS
    f  Recettes en devises
    d  Deviseneinnahmen

1476 FOREIGN EXCHANGE
    CONTROL
    f  Contrôle des changes
    d  Devisenbewirtschaftung

1477 FOREIGN EXCHANGE
    EXPENDITURES
    f  Dépenses en devises
    d  Devisenausgaben

1478 FOREIGN EXCHANGE
RESERVES
f  Montant des avoirs en
   devises
d  Devisenreserven

1479 SCARCITY OF FOREIGN
EXCHANGE
f  Pénurie de devises
d  Devisenknappheit

1480 FOREIGN PAYMENTS
f  Paiements extérieurs
d  Auslandszahlungen

1481 FOREIGN RESERVES
f  Avoirs extérieurs
d  Auslandsguthaben

1482 FUNDS ABROAD
f  Fonds à l'étranger
d  Auslandsfonds

1483 FUND FOR AID
f  Fonds d'aide
d  Hilfsfonds

1484 EARMARKED FUNDS
f  Fonds alloués;
   Affectation des fonds
d  Zweckgebundene Mittel

1485 PUBLIC FUNDS
f  Fonds publiques
d  Öffentliche Mittel

1486 SINKING FUND
f  Fonds d'amortissement
d  Amortisationsfonds

1487 INTEREST RATES
f  Taux d'intérêt
d  Zinssätze

1488 INVESTMENTS ABROAD
f  Investissements à
   l'étranger
d  Auslandsinvestitionen

1489 INVESTMENT ACTS
f  Législation relative à
   l'investissement

d  Investitionsgesetz-
   gebung

1490 INVESTMENT CLIMATE
f  Climat d'investissements
d  Investitionsklima

1491 INVESTMENT CRITERIA
f  Critères d'investissement
d  Investitionskriterien

1492 INVESTMENT EVALUATION
f  Evaluation des investissements
d  Investitionsschätzung

1493 INVESTMENT LAWS
f  Code des investissements
d  Investitionskodex

1494 INVESTMENT PLAN
f  Plan d'investissements
d  Investitionsplan

1495 INVESTMENT PLANNING
f  Planification de l'investissement
d  Investitionsplanung

1496 INVESTMENT POLICY
f  Politique d'investissement
d  Investitionspolitik

1497 INVESTMENT PRIORITIES
f  Priorités d'investissement
d  Investitionsprioritäten

1498 INVESTMENT PROGRAMME
f  Programme d'investissements
d  Investitionsprogramm

1499 INVESTMENT PROGRAM-
MING
f  Elaboration des programmes d'investissements
d  Ausarbeitung von
   Investitionsprogrammen

1500 INVESTMENT RATIO
f  Taux d'investissement
d  Investitionsrate

1501 INVESTMENT VARIANTS
f  Variantes d'investissements
d  Investitionsvarianten

1502 COMPLEMENTARY
INVESTMENTS
f  Investissements complémentaires
d  Komplementärinvestitionen

1503 DESINVESTMENT;
NEGATIVE INVESTMENT
f  Désinvestissement
d  Fehlinvestition;
   Negative Investition

1504 EXTRA-BUDGETING
INVESTMENTS
f  Investissements extra-
   budgétaires
d  Ausserbudgetäre
   Investitionen

1505 INVESTMENT FINANCING
f  Financement des inves-
   tissements
d  Investitionsfinanzierung

1506 FOREIGN INVESTMENTS
f  Investissements étrangers
d  Auslandsinvestitionen

1507 PREINVESTMENT AID
f  Aide au préinvestissement
d  Vorinvestitionshilfe

1508 PRIVATE INVESTMENTS
f  Investissements privés
d  Private Investitionen

1509 PRODUCTIVE INVESTMENTS
f  Investissements productifs
d  Produktive Investitionen

1510 PUBLIC INVESTMENTS
f  Investissements publics
d  Öffentliche Investitionen

1511 SOCIAL INVESTMENTS
f  Investissements sociaux
d  Soziale Investitionen

1512 SOCIAL INVESTMENT
PROJECT
f  Projet d'investissement
   social
d  Soziales Investitions-
   projekt

1513 ABILITY TO INVEST
f  Capacité d'investir
d  Investitionsfähigkeit

1514 CONTROL OF INVESTMENT
f  Contrôle de l'investissement
d  Investitionskontrolle

1515 LEVEL OF INVESTMENT
f  Niveau des investisse-
   ments
d  Investitionsniveau

1516 PROTECTION OF FOREIGN
INVESTMENT
f  Protection des investissements extérieures
d  Schutz der Auslands-
   investitionen

1517 SELECTION OF INVESTMENT
PROJECTS
f  Choix des projets
   d'investissements
d  Auswahl der Investitions-
   projekte

1518 INTERSECTORAL ALLO-
CATION OF INVESTMENTS
f  Allocation inter-secteur
   des investissements
d  Intersektorielle Verteilung
   der Investitionen

1519 COMMERCIAL INVESTORS
f  Investisseurs commer-
   ciaux
d  Kommerzielle Investoren

1520 FOREIGN INVESTORS
OF CAPITAL
f Apporteurs de capitaux
étrangers;
Investeurs de capitaux
étrangers
d Auslandsinvestoren

1521 LIABILITIES
f Passif
d Passiva

1522 LIQUIDITY POSITION
f Disponibilités en
liquidités
d Liquiditätssituation

1523 INTERNATIONAL LIQUIDITY
f Liquidité internationale
d Internationale Liquidität

1524 LOAN ADMINISTRATION
f Administration des prêts
d Kreditverwaltung

1525 LOAN CONTRACT
f Contrat de prêt
d Anleihevertrag

1526 ASSISTANCE LOANS
f Assistance au crédit
d Hilfskredite

1527 BANK LOANS
f Prêts bancaires
d Bankanleihen

1528 PUBLIC LOANS
f Emprunts publics
d Öffentliche Anleihen

1529 REPAYABLE LOAN
f Crédit remboursable
d Rückzahlbarer Kredit

1530 SOFT LOANS
f Prêts à taux de faveur
d Vorzugszinsen

1531 TIED LOAN
f Prêt à clause restrictive;

Prêt lié
d Gebundener Kredit

1532 FORMS OF LOANS
f Formes d'emprunts
d Anleiheformen

1533 "LUMPINESS" OF AN
INVESTMENT
f Indivisibilité d'un
investissement
d Unteilbarkeit einer
Investition

1534 MATERIAL MEANS
f Moyens matériels
d Materielle Mittel

1535 MONETARY AREA
f Zone monétaire
d Monetäre Zone

1536 MONETARY COOPERATION
f Coopération monétaire
d Monetäre Kooperation

1537 MONETARY EQUILIBRIUM
f Equilibre monétaire
d Monetäres Gleichgewicht

1538 MONETARY MATTERS
f Domaine monétaire
d Monetäre Angelegenheiten

1539 MONETARY OPERATIONS
f Opérations monétaires
d Monetäre Operationen

1540 MONETARY SITUATION
f Situation monétaire
d Monetäre Situation

1541 MONETARY STABILIZATION
f Stabilisation monétaire
d Monetäre Stabilisierung

1542 MONETIZE;
KETTRIDGE
f Monétiser
d Einschluss in die
Geldwirtschaft

1543    MONEY CAPITAL
      f   Capital monétaire
      d   Geldkapital

1544    MONEY MARKET
      f   Marché monétaire
      d   Geldmarkt

1545    CREATION OF MONEY
      f   Création de monnaie
      d   Geldschöpfung

1546    VOLUME OF MONEY
      f   Masse monétaire
      d   Geldvolumen

1547    MORTGAGE
      f   Crédit hypothécaire
      d   Hypothekärer Kredit

1548    GRACE PERIOD
      f   Délai de grace
      d   Moratorium;
         Stundung

1549    HOARDING
      f   Thésaurisation;
         Constitution de réserves
      d   Thesaurierung

1550    IMPORT SAVINGS
      f   Economies en devises
      d   Deviseneinsparungen

1551    EXTERNAL INCOMES
      f   Apports extérieurs
      d   Externe Einkommen

1552    MONEY INCOMES
      f   Ressources monétaires
      d   Monetäre Einkommen

1553    FINANCIAL INDUCEMENTS
      f   Stimulants financiers
      d   Finanzielle Stimuli

1554    INFLATION DANGER
      f   Danger inflationniste
      d   Inflationsgefahr

1555    CREEPING INFLATION
      f   Inflation latente
      d   Schleichende Inflation

1556    RUN-AWAY INFLATION
      f   Inflation en cours
      d   Galoppierende Inflation

1557    INFLATIONARY GAP
      f   Ecart inflationniste
      d   Inflationslücke

1558    INFLATIONARY PROPENSITY
      f   Propension à inflation
      d   Inflationsneigung

1559    INFLATIONARY PROCESS
      f   Processus inflatoire
      d   Inflationsprozess

1560    INFLATIONARY TENSIONS
      f   Tensions inflationnistes
      d   Inflationstendenzen

1561    DISINFLATIONARY
      f   Anti-inflationniste
      d   Anti-inflationär

1562    INTEREST PAYMENTS
      f   Versements d'intérêts
      d   Zinsenzahlung

1563    COMPOUND INTEREST
      f   Intérêts composés
      d   Zinseszinsen

1564    PENALTY INTEREST
      f   Intérêt de retard
      d   Verzugszinsen

1565    PATTERN OF SPENDING
      f   Structure des dépenses
      d   Ausgabenstruktur

1566    PAYING CAPACITY
      f   Capacité de paiement
      d   Zahlungsfähigkeit

1567    MEANS OF PAYMENT
      f   Moyens de paiement
      d   Zahlungsmittel

1568 METHODS OF PAYMENT
   f  Modalités de paiement
   d  Zahlungsmodalitäten

1569 PAYOFF PERIOD
   f  Période d'amortissement
   d  Amortisationsperiode

1570 PECUNIARY ECONOMIES
   f  Epargnes monétaires
   d  Monetäre Ersparnisse;
      Geldersparnisse

1571 PENNY CAPITALISM
   f  Capitalisme de sous
   d  Penny-Kapitalismus

1572 PRICE FORMATION
   f  Formation des prix
   d  Preisbildung

1573 PRICE INCREASE
   f  Augmentation des prix
   d  Preiserhöhung

1574 PRICE LEVEL
   f  Niveau des prix
   d  Preisniveau

1575 ACCOUNTING PRICE
   f  Prix comptable
   d  Rechnungspreis

1576 AVERAGE SELLING PRICE
   f  Prix de vente moyen
   d  Durchschnittlicher
      Verkaufspreis

1577 KEY PRICE
   f  Prix clef
   d  Schlüsselpreis

1578 MARKET PRICE
   f  Prix du marché
   d  Marktpreis

1579 OVER-PRICE
   f  Surprix
   d  Überpreis

1580 PARITY PRICE
   f  Prix de parité
   d  Paritätspreis

1581 SHADOW PRICE
   f  Prix fictif
   d  Fiktiver Preis

1582 DEVELOPMENT OF PRICES
   f  Evolution des prix
   d  Preisentwicklung

1583 ESTABLISHMENT OF
   PRICES UNDER PLANNING
   f  Formation des prix en
      système planifié
   d  Preisbildung in einer
      Planwirtschaft

1584 PRICING
   f  Détermination des prix
   d  Preisfestsetzung

1585 PRICING SYSTEM
   f  Régime des prix
   d  Preissystem

1586 PREINVESTMENT
   f  Pré-investissement
   d  Vorinvestition

1587 PROPENSITY TO SAVE
   f  Propension à épargner
   d  Sparneigung

1588 EARMARKED RECEIPTS
   f  Recettes affectées
   d  Gebundene Einnahmen

1589 REIMBURSEMENT BASIS
   f  Conditions de rembourse-
      ment
   d  Rückzahlungsbasis

1590 REIMBURSEMENT PERIOD;
   REPAYMENT PERIOD
   f  Période de rembourse-
      ment
   d  Rückzahlungsperiode

1591　TERMS AND CONDITIONS
OF REPAYMENT
f　Modalités de rembourse-
ment
d　Rückzahlungsmodus

1592　RESOURCE ALLOCATION
f　Allocation des ressources;
Répartition des ressources
d　Verteilung der Reserven

1593　NON-MONETARY
RESOURCES
f　Ressources non-moné-
taires
d　Nicht-monetäre Reserven

1594　AVERAGE REVENUE
f　Recette moyenne
d　Durchschnittliches
Einkommen

1595　MARGINAL REVENUE
f　Recette marginale
d　Marginales Einkommen;
Grenzeinkommen

1596　PUBLIC REVENUES
f　Recettes publiques
d　Öffentliche Einnahmen

1597　SAVINGS RATIO
f　Taux de l'épargne
d　Sparrate

1598　DISSAVINGS
f　Epargne négative;
Déségargnes
d　Negative Ersparnisse

1599　DOMESTIC SAVINGS;
LOCAL SAVINGS
f　Epargne intérieure
d　Lokale Ersparnisse

1600　GROSS SAVINGS
f　Epargne brute
d　Bruttoersparnisse

1601　HOUSEHOLD SAVINGS
f　Epargne des ménages
d　Ersparnisse der Haushalte

1602　STOCK EXCHANGE
f　Bourse
d　Börse

1603　SUBSIDIES;
GRANTS IN AID
f　Subventions
d　Subventionen

1604　TYPE OF TRANSACTION
f　Type de transaction
d　Transaktionsart

1605　TRANSFER OPERATIONS
f　Opérations de transfert
d　Transfertoperationen

1606　TRANSFER PAYMENTS
f　Paiements de transfert
d　Transferzahlungen;
Zahlungsverkehr

1607　RATE OF CAPITAL
TURNOVER
f　Vitesse de rotation du
capital
d　Umlaufgeschwindigkeit
des Kapitals

1608　USES
f　Emplois
d　Verwendung

1609　COUNTER-VALUE
f　Contre-valeur
d　Gegenwert

1610　UNIT VALUE
f　Valeur unitaire
d　Einheitswert

1611　USE-VALUE
f　Valeur d'usage
d　Gebrauchswert

1612　PRIVATE WEALTH
f　Patrimoine privé
d　Privates Vermögen

# VII.

## FINANCE AND TAXES
## FINANCE ET FISCALITE
## FINANZ UND FISKALITÄT

1613 BALANCE SHEETS OF
BANKING INSTITUTIONS
f Bilans bancaires
d Bank-Bilanzen

1614 BANK UNION
f Union des banques
d Bankunion

1615 AGRICULTURAL BANK
f Banque de l'agriculture
d Landwirtschaftsbank

1616 CENTRAL BANK
f Banque centrale
d Zentralbank

1617 CENTRAL ISSUING BANK
f Banque centrale
d'émission
d Notenbank

1618 COMMERCIAL BANK
f Banque commerciale
d Handelsbank

1619 COOPERATIVE BANK
f Banque coopérative
d Genossenschaftsbank

1620 DEPOSIT BANK
f Banque de dépôts
d Depositenbank

1621 DEVELOPMENT BANK
f Banque de développement
d Entwicklungsbank

1622 FOREIGN TRADE BANK
f Banque du commerce
extérieur
d Aussenhandelsbank

1623 GOVERNMENT BANK
f Banque publique
d Staatsbank

1624 INDUSTRIAL BANK
f Banque industrielle
d Industriebank

1625 MUNICIPAL BANK
f Banque municipale
d Kommunalbank

1626 NATIONAL INVESTMENT
BANK
f Banque nationale
d'investissements
d Nationale Investitions-
bank

1627 PRIVATE BANK
f Banque privée
d Privatbank

1628 SAVING BANK
f Caisse d'épargne
d Sparkasse

1629 SEMI-PRIVATE BANK
f Banque semi-publique
d Halbstaatliche Bank

1630 STRUCTURE OF THE BANK
f Structure de la banque
d Struktur der Bank

1631 BANKING
f Banques
d Banken

1632 BANKING INSTITUTION
f Institut bancaire
d Bankinstitut

1633 BANKING LAWS
f Législation bancaire
d Bankgesetzgebung

1634 BANKING OPERATIONS
f Opérations bancaires
d Bankgeschäfte

1635 BANKING ORGANIZATION
f Organisation bancaire
d Bankorganisation

1636 BANKING STRUCTURE
f Structure bancaire
d Bankstruktur

1637 BANKING SYSTEM
f Système bancaire
d Banksystem

1638 TYPE OF BANKING INSTI-
TUTE
f Catégorie de banques
d Bankkategorie

1639 BUDGET ESTIMATE
f Estimation budgétaire
d Budgetvoranschlag

1640 DRAFT BUDGET
f Projet de budget
d Budgetentwurf

1641 FAMILY BUDGET;
FAMILY INCOME AND
EXPENDITURE
f Budget familial
d Familienbudget

1642 MILITARY BUDGET
f Budget militaire
d Militärbudget

1643 NATIONAL ECONOMIC
BUDGET
f Budget économique
national
d Nationales Wirtschafts-
budget

1644 ORDINARY BUDGET
f Budget général
d Allgemeines Budget

1645 SPECIAL BUDGET
f Budget spécial
d Sonderbudget

1646 PREPARATION OF THE
BUDGET
f Préparation du budget
d Budgetvorbereitung

1647 BUDGETARY EXPENDITURE
f Dépenses budgétaires
d Budgetausgaben

1648 BUDGETARY RECEIPTS
f Recettes budgétaires
d Budgeteinnahmen

1649 BUDGETARY YEAR
f Année budgétaire
d Finanzjahr

1650 CLEARING SYSTEM
f Système de clearing
d Clearingsystem

1651 COST OF COLLECTING
f Coût de perception
d Einhebungskosten

1652 BALKANISATION OF CREDIT
f Balkanisation du crédit
d Balkanisierung des
Kredites

1653 CURRENCY BOARD
f Banque d'émission
d Emissionsbank

1654 CURRENCY REFORM;
MONETARY REFORM
f Réforme monétaire
d Währungsreform

1655 CONVERTIBLE CURRENCY
f Devises convertibles
d Konvertible Devisen

1656 FOREIGN CURRENCY
f   Monnaie étrangère
d   Auslandswährung

1657 FOREIGN CURRENCY
RESERVES
f   Réserves de devises
d   Devisenreserven

1658 HARD CURRENCY
f   Devise forte;
Monnaie forte
d   Harte Währung

1659 HOME CURRENCY;
LOCAL CURRENCY
f   Monnaie locale
d   Inlandswährung

1660 KEY CURRENCIES
f   Monnaies-clef
d   Schlüsselwährungen

1661 NATIONAL CURRENCY
f   Monnaie nationale
d   Nationale Währung;
Eigene Währung

1662 SOFT CURRENCY
f   Monnaie faible
d   Weiche Währung

1663 WORLD CURRENCIES
f   Monnaies mondiales
d   Weltwährungen

1664 DEVALUATION OF THE
CURRENCY
f   Dévalutation monétaire
d   Währungsabwertung

1665 LOSS OF FOREIGN
CURRENCY
f   Perte de devises
d   Devisenverlust

1666 DEPRECIATION
f   Dépréciation
d   Entwertung

1667 DEVALUATION
f   Dévaluation
d   Abwertung

1668 DISCOUNT RATE
f   Taux d'escompte
d   Diskontsatz

1669 DRAWBACK
f   Ristourne;
Draw-back
d   Steuerrückvergütung

1670 AD VALOREM DUTY
f   Droit ad valorem
d   Wertsteuer

1671 PROTECTIVE DUTY
f   Droit protecteur
d   Schutzzoll

1672 FOREIGN EXCHANGE
POLICY
f   Politique des devises
d   Devisenpolitik

1673 MULTIPLE EXCHANGE
RATES
f   Multiplicité des taux
de change
d   Multipler Wechselkurs

1674 EXPENDITURES AND
RECEIPTS
f   Dépenses et recettes
d   Ausgaben und Einnahmen

1675 TREASURY EXPENDITURE
f   Dépenses de trésorerie
d   Finanzausgaben

1676 FINANCIAL CRISIS
f   Crise financière
d   Finanzkrise

1677 FINANCIAL ECONOMY
f   Economie financière
d   Finanzwirtschaft

1678 FINANCIAL INSTITUTIONS;
　　 FINANCIAL COMPANIES
　　 f　Sociétés financières
　　 d　Finanzgesellschaften

1679 FINANCIAL MEANS
　　 f　Moyens financiers
　　 d　Finanzmittel

1680 FINANCIAL PERIOD
　　 f　Exercice financier
　　 d　Finanzperiode

1681 FINANCIAL PLANNING
　　 f　Planification financière
　　 d　Finanzplanung

1682 FISCAL SYSTEM
　　 f　Régime fiscal
　　 d　Steuersystem

1683 FLEXIBILITY IN
　　 TRANSACTIONS
　　 f　Souplesse dans les
　　　　transactions
　　 d　Beweglichkeit in den
　　　　Transaktionen

1684 GOVERNMENT DEBTS
　　 f　Dettes de l'Etat
　　 d　Staatsschulden

1685 FISCAL ADMINISTRATION
　　 f　Administration fiscale
　　 d　Fiskalische Verwaltung

1686 FISCAL ADVISER
　　 f　Spécialiste des questions
　　　　monétaires et fiscales
　　 d　Finanzberater

1687 FISCAL POLICY
　　 f　Politique fiscale;
　　　　Politique financière
　　 d　Finanzpolitik

1688 FISCAL REGIME
　　 f　Régime fiscal
　　 d　Fiskalsystem

1689 FISCAL THEORY
　　 f　Science des finances;
　　　　Science financière
　　 d　Finanzwissenschaft

1690 FINANCE BILL
　　 f　Loi de finance
　　 d　Finanzgesetz

1691 INTERNATIONAL FINANCE
　　 f　Finances internationales
　　 d　Internationale Finanzen

1692 LOCAL FINANCE
　　 f　Finances locales
　　 d　Lokale Finanzen

1693 PUBLIC FINANCE
　　 f　Finances publiques
　　 d　Öffentliches Finanz-
　　　　wesen;
　　　　Öffentliche Finanzen

1694 SOURCE OF FINANCE
　　 f　Source de financement
　　 d　Finanzquelle

1695 DEFICIT OF FINANCING
　　 f　Déficit de financement
　　 d　Finanzdefizit

1696 FINANCIAL ADMINI-
　　 STRATION;
　　 FINANCIAL MANAGEMENT
　　 f　Administration financière;
　　　　Gestion financière
　　 d　Finanzielle Verwaltung

1697 FINANCIAL BALANCE
　　 SHEET
　　 f　Bilan financier
　　 d　Finanzbilanz

1698 LABOUR SERVICE
　　 f　Impôt en travail
　　 d　Arbeitsdienst

1699 LOSS OF CAPITAL
　　 f　Fuite de capitaux
　　 d　Kapitalflucht

1700 MONETARY AGREEMENT
   f Accord monétaire
   d Währungsabkommen

1701 MONETARY POLICY
   f Politique monétaire
   d Währungspolitik

1702 MONETARY SYSTEM
   f Système monétaire
   d Monetäres System

1703 MONETARY UNION
   f Union monétaire
   d Währungsunion

1704 MONETARY UNIT
   f Unité monétaire
   d Währungseinheit

1705 STABLE MONETARY
   CONDITIONS
   f Stabilité monétaire
   d Währungsstabilität

1706 NETWORK OF FINANCIAL
   INSTITUTIONS
   f Réseau d'établissements
     financiers
   d Netz von Finanzierungs-
     institutionen

1707 OVER-GRADING
   f Surestimation;
     Surévaluation;
     Surclassement
   d Überbewertung

1708 PARITY
   f Parité
   d Parität

1709 PAYMENTS IN KIND
   f Prestations en nature
   d Abgaben in Gütern;
     Naturalabgaben

1710 PURCHASING POWER;
   BUYING POWER
   f Pouvoir d'achat
   d Kaufkraft

1711 REVALORIZATION
   f Revalorisation
   d Aufwertung

1712 ROYALTIES ON NATURAL
   RESOURCES
   f Redevances afférantes
     à l'exploitation de
     ressources naturelles
   d Lizenzgebühr für den
     Abbau von Bodenschätzen;
     Ertragsanteil für Boden-
     schätze

1713 SHADOW RATE
   f Taux fictif;
     Taux comptable
   d Fiktive Rate

1714 SOURCE OF REVENUE
   f Ressource fiscale
   d Steuerquelle

1715 STABILIZATION FUND
   f Caisse de stabilisation
   d Stabilisierungskasse

1716 STABILITY OF PRICES
   f Stabilité de prix
   d Preisstabilität

1717 SUPPLY OF FOREIGN
   CAPITAL
   f Apports de capitaux
     étrangers
   d Angebot an Auslands-
     kapital

1718 SURTAX
   f Surtaxe
   d Steuerzusatz

1719 TAX AUTHORITIES
   f Autorités fiscales
   d Steuerbehörden

1720 TAX BARRIERS
   f Barrières fiscales
   d Steuerschranken

1721 TAX ADMINISTRATION
    f  Administration fiscale
    d  Steuerverwaltung

1722 TAX AGREEMENT
    f  Accord fiscal
    d  Steuerabkommen

1723 TAX BASE
    f  Assiette de l'impôt
    d  Steuerbasis

1724 TAX BURDEN
    f  Pression fiscale
    d  Steuerdruck

1725 TAX CHANGES
    f  Modification du système
       fiscale
    d  Steueränderung

1726 TAX COLLECTING
    f  Perception de l'impôt
    d  Steuereinhebung

1727 TAX COLLECTING
    MACHINERY
    f  Appareil de perception
       des impôts
    d  Steuereinhebungsapparat

1728 TAX DISCRIMINATION
    f  Discrimination fiscale
    d  Steuerliche Diskriminie-
       rung

1729 TAX ENFORCEMENT;
    INTERNATIONAL REVENUE
    CONTROL
    f  Contrôle fiscal
    d  Fiskalische Kontrolle;
       Steuerkontrolle

1730 TAX EVASION;
    FISCAL EVASION
    f  Evasion fiscale
    d  Steuerflucht

1731 TAX FREE INCOME
    f  Revenu exempté
    d  Steuerfreies Einkommen

1732 TAX IMMUNITIES
    f  Immunités fiscales
    d  Steuerimmunität

1733 TAX JURISDICTION
    f  Juridiction fiscale
    d  Steuergesetzgebung

1734 TAX LAW
    f  Loi fiscale
    d  Steuergesetz

1735 TAX MEASURES
    f  Mesures fiscales
    d  Steuermassnahmen

1736 TAX MORALITY
    f  Morale fiscale
    d  Steuermoral

1737 TAX SPECIALIST
    f  Expert fiscal;
       Expert en matière
       d'impôt
    d  Steuerexperte

1738 TAX STRUCTURE
    f  Structure de l'impôt
    d  Steuerstruktur

1739 TAX SYSTEM;
    SYSTEM OF TAXATION
    f  Système de taxation;
       Système fiscal
    d  Steuersystem

1740 DIRECT TAX
    f  Impôt direct;
       Contribution directe
    d  Direkte Steuer

1741 EXCISE TAX;
    EXCISE DUTY
    f  Droits de régie
    d  Verbrauchssteuer

1742 EXPORT TAX
    f  Taxe à l'exportation;
       Droits de sortie
    d  Exportsteuer

743 FIXED TAX
   f Tax forfaitaire
   d Pauschalsteuer

744 HEAD TAX
   f Impôt sur la personne
   d Kopfsteuer

745 IMPORT TAX
   f Taxe à l'importation;
     Droits d'entrée
   d Importsteuer

746 TAX PAYING CAPACITY
   f Capacité contributive
     individuelle
   d Steuerzahlungsfähigkeit

747 TAX POLICY
   f Politique fiscale
   d Steuerpolitik

748 TAX RATE
   f Taux de l'impôt
   d Steuersatz

749 TAX RECEIPTS
   f Recettes d'impôts;
     Recettes fiscales
   d Steuereinnahmen

1750 TAX REDUCTION
   f Réduction d'impôt
   d Steuerreduktion

1751 TAX REFORM
   f Réforme fiscale
   d Steuerreform

1752 TAX RELIEF;
   TAX REBATE
   f Détaxe;
     Dégrèvement
   d Steuernachlass

1753 TAX REVENUE
   f Revenus fiscaux
   d Steuereinkommen

1754 INDIRECT TAX
   f Impôt indirect;

   Contribution indirecte
   d Indirekte Steuer

1755 LAND TAX
   f Impôt foncier;
     Impôt sur la terre
   d Grundsteuer

1756 LOCAL TAX;
   MUNICIPAL TAX
   f Impôt local
   d Örtliche Steuer

1757 LUXURY TAX
   f Impôt sur les articles
     de luxe;
     Taxe de luxe
   d Luxussteuer

1758 POLL TAX
   f Imposition de capitation
   d Kopfsteuer

1759 PROPERTY TAX
   f Impôt sur la fortune
   d Vermögenssteuer

1760 PURCHASE TAX;
   SALES TAX
   f Impôt de consommation
   d Konsumsteuer

1761 TURNOVER TAX
   f Taxe sur le chiffre
     d'affaires
   d Umsatzsteuer

1762 WAGE TAX;
   PAYROLL TAX
   f Prélèvement sur les
     salariés
   d Lohnsteuer

1763 ZAKAT-TAX
   f Taxe "zakat"
   d Zakat-Steuer

1764 SHIFTING OF THE TAX
   f Répercussion de l'impôt
   d Steuerüberwälzung

92

1765 YIELD OF A TAX
  f  Rendement d'un impôt
  d  Steuerertrag

1766 TAXABLE INCOME
  f  Revenu imposable
  d  Besteuerbares Einkommen

1767 TAXATION
  f  Fiscalité
  d  Steuerwesen

1768 TAXATION PER HEAD;
  TAXATION PER CAPITA
  f  Prélèvement fiscale
     "per capita"
  d  Kopfbesteuerung;
     Pro-Kopf Besteuerung

1769 TAXATION SCHEDULE
  f  Tarif de l'impôt
  d  Steuertarif

1770 AGRICULTURAL TAXATION
  f  Fiscalité agricole
  d  Agrarfiskalität

1771 DOUBLE IMPOSITION;
  DOUBLE TAXATION
  f  Double imposition;
     Double taxation
  d  Doppelbesteuerung

1772 DOUBLE TAXATION AGREE-
  MENT
  f  Convention relative aux
     doubles impositions
  d  Doppelbesteuerungsabkom-
     men

1773 DOUBLE TAXATION
  RELIEF
  f  Double dégrèvement
     d'impôts
  d  Befreiung von Doppel-
     besteuerung

1774 PRESUMPTIVE TAXATION
  f  Imposition forfaitaire
  d  Pauschalbesteuerung

1775 UNREALISTIC
  TAXATION
  f  Imposition peu réaliste
  d  Unrealistische
     Besteuerung

1776 METHOD OF TAXATION;
  TAXATION METHOD
  f  Mode d'imposition
  d  Besteuerungsmethode

1777 PATTERN OF TAXATION
  f  Structure de la fiscalité
  d  Steuerstruktur

1778 SYSTEM OF TAXATION
  f  Régime fiscal
  d  Besteuerungssystem

1779 TAXING POWER
  f  Droit d'imposer
  d  Besteuerungsrecht

# VIII.
## TRADE
## COMMERCE
## HANDEL

'80 SPECIALIZED AGENCIES
f Institutions spécialisées
d Spezialorganisationen

'81 AGREEMENT SCHEME
f Projet d'accord
d Abkommensschema

'82 AGREEMENT FOR COMPENSATION; COMPENSATION AGREEMENT
f Accord de compensation
d Kompensationsabkommen

'83 AGREEMENT ON COOPERATION
f Accord de coopération
d Kooperationsabkommen

84 AGREEMENT ON TRADE
f Convention commerciale
d Handelsabkommen

85 BILATERAL AGREEMENT
f Accord bilatéral
d Bilaterales Abkommen

86 COMMERCIAL AGREEMENT
f Accord commercial
d Handelsabkommen

87 COMMODITY AGREEMENT
f Accord sur les produits de base
d Rohstoffabkommen

88 INTERNATIONAL AGREEMENT
f Accord international
d Internationales Abkommen

1789 LONG-TERM AGREEMENT
f Accord à long terme
d Langfristiges Abkommen

1790 MULTILATERAL PAYMENT AGREEMENT
f Accord de paiement multilatéral
d Multilaterales Zahlungsabkommen

1791 MUTUAL AGREEMENT
f Accord mutuel
d Gegenseitiges Abkommen

1792 TRADE AGREEMENT; TRADING AGREEMENT
f Accord commercial; Convention commerciale
d Handelsabkommen

1793 TRANSIT AGREEMENT
f Accord de transit
d Transitabkommen

1794 TEXT OF AGREEMENT
f Texte de l'accord
d Text des Abkommens

1795 AID AND TRADE
f Aide et échange
d Hilfe und Handel

1796 FORMS OF AID
f Formes d'aide
d Hilfsformen

1797 NATURAL SOURCES OF AID
f Sources naturelles d'aide
d Natürliche Hilfsquellen

1798 ASSOCIATION CONVENTION
f Convention d'association
d Assoziierungsabkommen

1799 SUPRA-NATIONAL
AUTHORITY
f Autorité supra-nationale
d Supranationale Behörde

1800 BALANCE OF TRADE
f Balance commerciale
d Handelsbilanz

1801 FAVOURABLE BALANCE
OF TRADE
f Balance commerciale
excédentale
d Aktive Handelsbilanz

1802 BARGAINING POWER
f Pouvoir de négociation
d Verhandlungsstärke

1803 COLLECTIVE BARGAINING
f Négociations collectives
d Gemeinsame Verhand-
lungen

1804 BUFFER-STOCKS
f Stocks-tampons
d Buffer-Stocks

1805 BUSINESS STRUCTURE
f Structure des affaires
d Geschäftsstruktur

1806 CATEGORY OF COMMER-
CIAL ACTIVITY
f Catégorie d'activité
commerciale
d Kategorie der Handels-
tätigkeit

1807 CATEGORY OF MERCHAN-
DISE
f Catégorie de marchan-
dises
d Kategorie der Waren

1808 COMMERCE BY
MONETARY ZONES
f Commerce par zones
monétaires
d Handel nach monetären
Zonen

1809 COMMERCIAL AGRI-
CULTURAL PRODUCTION
f Production agricole
commerciale
d Kommerzielle Agrar-
produktion

1810 COMMERCIAL DEFICIT
f Déficit commercial
d Handelsdefizit

1811 COMMERCIAL ECONOMY
f Economie mercantile
d Handelswirtschaft

1812 COMMERCIAL
EXPLOITATION
f Exploitation commerciale
d Kommerzielle Ausbeutung

1813 COMMERCIAL FACILITIES
f Facilités commerciales
d Handelserleichterungen

1814 COMMERCIAL ORGANI-
ZATION
f Organisation commerci-
ale
d Handelsorganisation

1815 COMMERCIAL POLICY
f Politique commerciale
d Handelspolitik

1816 COMMERCIAL POSITION
f Position commerciale
d Handelsposition

1817 COMMERCIAL PROFITA-
BILITY
f Rentabilité commerciale
d Handelsprofit

1818 COMMERCIAL PROSPECTS
    f  Perspectives commerci-
      ales
    d  Handelsaussichten

1819 COMMERCIAL RELATIONS
    f  Relations commerciales
    d  Handelsbeziehungen

1820 COMMODITY
    f  Produit
    d  Produkt;
      Gut

1821 COMMODITY GROUPS
    f  Groupes de produits
    d  Warengruppen

1822 LUXURY COMMODITY
    f  Article de luxe
    d  Luxusgut

1823 COMPARATIVE
    ADVANTAGES
    f  Avantages comparés
    d  Komparative Vorteile

1824 COMPENSATING CHANGE
    f  Changement compensa-
      toire
    d  Austauschkompensation

1825 PERFECT COMPETITION
    f  Concurrence parfaite
    d  Vollkommene Konkurrenz

1826 THREATS OF COMPETITION
    f  Menace de concurrence
    d  Konkurrenzgefahr

1827 COMPETITIVE POSITION
    f  Position concurrentielle
    d  Konkurrenzposition;
      Konkurrenzstellung

1828 COMPETITORS
    f  Concurrents
    d  Konkurrenten

1829 CONVERSION OF
    PRODUCTION
    f  Reconversion de la
      production
    d  Umstellung der
      Produktion

1830 COUNTRY OF RAW
    MATERIALS
    f  Pays de matières
      premières
    d  Rohstoffland

1831 "DEFICIT COUNTRY"
    f  "Pays déficitaire"
    d  "Defizitland"

1832 PARTNER COUNTRY;
    MEMBER COUNTRY
    f  Pays partenaire
    d  Partnerland

1833 RECIPIENT COUNTRY;
    COUNTRY OF DESTI-
    NATION
    f  Pays de destination
    d  Bestimmungsland

1834 "SURPLUS COUNTRY"
    f  "Pays excédentaire"
    d  "Überschussland"

1835 SUPPLYING COUNTRY
    f  Pays fournisseur
    d  Lieferland

1836 CUSTOMERS
    f  Clients
    d  Kunden

1837 CUSTOMS
    f  Douanes
    d  Zollwesen

1838 CUSTOMS ARRANGEMENTS
    f  Régimes douaniers
    d  Zollabkommen

1839 CUSTOMS DUTIES
    f  Droits de douane
    d  Zollabgaben

1840 CUSTOMS FORMALITIES;
     TARIFFS FORMALITIES
     f  Formalités douanières;
        Formalités tarifaires
     d  Zollformalitäten

1841 CUSTOMS FRAUD
     f  Infraction douanière
     d  Zollhinterziehung

1842 CUSTOMS PROTECTION
     f  Protection douanière
     d  Zollschutz

1843 CUSTOMS REVENUE
     f  Recettes douanières
     d  Zolleinkünfte

1844 CUSTOMS SYSTEM
     f  Régime douanier
     d  Zollsystem

1845 CUSTOMS TARIFFS
     f  Tarifs douaniers
     d  Zolltarife

1846 CUSTOMS UNION
     f  Union douanière
     d  Zollunion

1847 DEFICIT OF THE COMMER-
     CIAL BALANCE
     f  Déficit de la balance
        commerciale
     d  Defizit der Handelsbilanz

1848 DECISION-MAKING CENTRES
     f  Centres de décision
     d  Entscheiderzentren

1849 EFFECTIVE DEMAND
     f  Demande effective
     d  Tatsächliche Nachfrage

1850 FINAL DEMAND
     f  Demande finale
     d  Endnachfrage

1851 INTERMEDIATE DEMAND
     f  Demande intermédiaire
     d  Zwischennachfrage

1852 POTENTIAL DEMAND
     f  Demande potentielle
     d  Potentielle Nachfrage

1853 RURAL DEMAND
     f  Demande rurale
     d  Nachfrage auf dem Land

1854 URBAN DEMAND
     f  Demande urbaine
     d  Städtische Nachfrage

1855 DISCRIMINATION
     f  Discrimination
     d  Diskriminierung

1856 DISTRIBUTION CHANNELS
     f  Réseau de distribution
     d  Verteilungsnetz

1857 DISTRIBUTION COST
     f  Coût de la distribution
     d  Verteilungskosten

1858 DISTRIBUTIONAL EFFECTS
     f  Effets de la distribution
     d  Verteilungseffekte

1859 DRAWBACK;
     REBATE
     f  Ristourne des droits
        de douane
     d  Zollrückvergütung

1860 HIDDEN DUMPING
     f  Dumping occulte
     d  Verstecktes Dumping

1861 ANTI-DUMPING MEASURES
     f  Mesures anti-dumping
     d  Anti-Dumping Mass-
        nahmen

1862 ECONOMIC UNION
     f  Union économique
     d  Wirtschaftsunion

1863 COMMERCIAL ECONOMY
     f  Economie mercantile
     d  Kommerzielle Wirtschaft

1864 INTERNATIONAL ECONOMY
f Economie internationale
d Internationale Wirtschaft

1865 WORLD ECONOMY
f Economie mondiale
d Weltwirtschaft

1866 EXCHANGE ARRANGEMENT
f Accord en matière de change
d Austauschabkommen

1867 EXCHANGE CONTROL
f Contrôle des changes
d Aussenhandelskontrolle

1868 INTERNATIONAL EXCHANGE
f Exchanges internationaux
d Internationaler Handels-austausch

1869 EXEMPTION FROM DUTY
f Franchise douanière
d Zollbefreiung

1870 TRAVELLING EXHIBITION
f Exposition itinérante
d Wanderausstellung

1871 EXPANSION OF EXPORTS
f Expansion des exporta-tions
d Exportfortschritt

1872 NATIONAL EXPANSION
f Expansion nationale
d Natürliche Expansion

1873 EXPORT BOUNTY
f Subvention à l'exportation
d Exportsubvention

1874 EXPORT CREDITS
f Crédits garantis à l'exportation
d Garantierte Exportkredite

1875 EXPORT EARNINGS
f Recettes d'exportation
d Exporteinnahmen

1876 EXPORT INDUSTRY
f Industrie d'exportation
d Exportindustrie

1877 EXPORT MARKET
f Marché d'exportation
d Exportmarkt

1878 EXPORT POSSIBILITIES
f Possibilités d'exporta-tion
d Exportmöglichkeiten

1879 EXPORT PRICE
f Prix à l'exportation
d Exportpreis

1880 EXPORT PRODUCTS
f Produits d'exportation
d Exportprodukte

1881 EXPORT PROSPECTS
f Perspectives d'expor-tation
d Exportchancen

1882 EXPORT QUOTA
f Contingent d'exportation
d Exportkontingent

1883 EXPORT ROUTES
f Circuits d'exportation
d Exportwege

1884 EXPORT SUBSIDY
f Prime à l'exportation
d Exportunterstützung

1885 EXPORT TRADE
f Commerce d'exportation
d Exporthandel

1886 EXPORT VOLUME
f Volume des exportations
d Exportvolumen

1887 INDUSTRIAL EXPORTS
f Exportations industrielles
d Industrieexporte

1888 INVISIBLE EXPORTS
    f  Exportations invisibles
    d  Unsichtbare Exporte

1889 IRREGULAR EXPORTS
    f  Exportations irrégulières
    d  Irreguläre Exporte

1890 NATURAL EXPORT
    MARKETS
    f  Marchés naturels d'ex-
       portation
    d  Natürliche Exportmärkte

1891 PRINCIPAL EXPORTS
    f  Principales exportations
    d  Hauptexporte

1892 RE-EXPORT
    f  Ré-exportation
    d  Re-Export

1893 TOTAL EXPORTS AND
    IMPORTS
    f  Totalité des exportations
       et des importations
    d  Gesamte Export- und
       Importbewegung

1894 TRADITIONAL EXPORTS
    f  Exportations tradition-
       nelles
    d  Traditionelle Exporte

1895 COMPOSITION OF EXPORTS
    f  Composition des
       exportations
    d  Exportstruktur

1896 FOREIGN SALES;
    SALES ABROAD
    f  Ventes à l'étranger
    d  Auslandsverkauf

1897 FOREIGN TRADE;
    EXTERNAL COMMERCE
    f  Commerce extérieur
    d  Aussenhandel

1898 FOREIGN TRADE BALANCE
    f  Balance commerciale
    d  Aussenhandelsbilanz

1899 FOREIGN TRADE
    MULTIPLIER
    f  Multiplicateur du
       commerce extérieur
    d  Aussenhandelsmulti-
       plikator

1900 FOREIGN TRADE
    RELATIONS
    f  Relations commerciales
       extérieures
    d  Aussenhandelsbeziehungen

1901 FRAUD
    f  Fraude
    d  Schmuggel

1902 FREE TRADE
    f  Libre-échange
    d  Freihandel

1903 FREE TRADE AREA
    f  Zone de libre échange
    d  Freihandelszone

1904 FREE PORT
    f  Port franc
    d  Freihafen

1905 FREEDOM OF CAPITAL
    TRANSFER
    f  Liberté du transfert
       des capitaux
    d  Freizügigkeit des
       Kapitaltransfers

1906 GLUT
    f  Offre excessive d'un
       produit
    d  Marktschwemme

1907 CAPITAL GOODS
    f  Biens d'équipement
    d  Kapitalgüter

1908 INTERMEDIATE GOODS
    f  Biens intermédiaires
    d  Halbfertigprodukte;
       Halbfertigfabrikate

1909 LIST OF GOODS
f Nomenclature des
marchandises
d Güterliste

1910 VOLUME OF GOODS
f Volume des marchandises
d Gütervolumen

1911 GOVERNMENT ORDERS
f Commandes administra-
tives
d Regierungsaufträge

1912 SUB-REGIONAL GROUPING
f Groupement sous-régional
d Subregionale Gruppierung

1913 HARMONIZATION
f Harmonisation
d Harmonisierung

1914 IMPORT LICENCE
f Licence d'importations
d Importlizenz

1915 IMPORT QUOTAS
f Contingents d'importation
d Importkontingente

1916 IMPORT REQUIREMENTS
f Besoins en importations
d Importerfordernisse

1917 IMPORT RESTRICTIONS
f Restrictions à
l'importation
d Importbeschränkungen

1918 IMPORT SUBSTITUTION
f Substition des
importations
d Importsubstitution;
Importersatz

1919 IMPORT SUBSTITUTION
POLICY
f Politique de substitution
des importations
d Importsubstitutions-
politik

1920 AGGREGATE IMPORTS
f Importations globales
d Gesamtimporte

1921 ALLOCATION OF THE
IMPORTS
f Répartition des
importations
d Verteilung der Importe

1922 DISTRIBUTION OF IMPORTS
f Répartition des
importations
d Importstruktur

1923 LEVEL OF IMPORTS
f Niveau des importations
d Importniveau

1924 TRENDS OF IMPORTS
f Evolution des
importations
d Importtrends

1925 IMPORT AND EXPORT
DEVELOPMENT
f Développement des
échanges
d Import- und Export-
entwicklung

1926 IMPORT AND EXPORT
LIBERALIZATION
f Libéralisation des
importations et ex-
portations
d Import- und Exportlibe-
ralisierung

1927 IMPORT-EXPORT POLICY
f Politique des échanges
d Import-Export Politik

1928 IMPORTER
f Importateur
d Importeur

1929 INTEGRATED AREA
f Zone intégrée
d Integrierte Zone

1930 INTERMEDIARIES
f Intermédiaires
d Zwischenhändler

1931 INTERREGIONAL ECONOMIC
RELATIONS
f Relations économiques
inter-régionales
d Interregionale Wirtschaftsbeziehungen

1932 INVENTORY EVALUATION
f Evaluation des stocks
d Inventarbewertung

1933 LEVELLING OFF OF
VOLUME OF IMPORTS
f Stabilisation du volume
des importations
d Stabilisierung des
Importvolumens

1934 LIBERALIZATION
f Libéralisation
d Liberalisierung

1935 LIBERALIZATION
PROBLEMS
f Problèmes de libérali-
sation
d Liberalisierungsprobleme

1936 MARKET CONDITIONS
f Conditions du marché
d Marktbedingungen

1937 MARKET FRAGMENTATION
f Fragmentation du marché
d Zerstückelung des
Marktes

1938 MARKET INFORMATION
f Information sur les
marchés
d Marktinformation

1939 MARKET ORGANIZATION
f Organisation des marchés
d Marktordnung

1940 MARKET PROSPECTS;
TONE OF THE MARKET
f Allure générale du
marché
d Marktlage

1941 MARKET SUPPLY
f Approvisionnement du
marché
d Marktversorgung

1942 MARKET SURVEY
f Etude des marchés
d Marktstudie

1943 MARKET TRENDS
f Tendances des marchés
d Markttendenzen

1944 MARKET FOR TROPICAL
PRODUCTS
f Marché des produits
tropicaux
d Markt für tropische
Produkte

1945 BLACK MARKET
f Marché noir
d Schwarzer Markt

1946 COFFEE MARKET
f Marché du café
d Kaffeemarkt

1947 COMMON MARKET
f Marché Commun
d Gemeinsamer Markt

1948 DOMESTIC MARKET
f Marché intérieur
d Binnenmarkt

1949 FOREIGN MARKET
f Marché extérieur
d Auslandsmarkt

HOME MARKET
f Marché intérieur
d Inlandsmarkt

1951 LOCAL MARKET
    f  Marché local
    d  Lokaler Markt;
       Lokalmarkt

1952 OUTLET MARKET
    f  Commerce de débouchés
    d  Absatzmarkt

1953 POTENTIAL MARKET
    f  Marché potentiel
    d  Potentieller Markt

1954 PROPERTY MARKET
    f  Marché immobilier
    d  Immobilienmarkt

1955 REGIONAL MARKET
    f  Marché régional
    d  Regionalmarkt

1956 RURAL MARKET
    f  Marché rural
    d  Agrarmarkt

1957 TEXTILE MARKET
    f  Marché du textile
    d  Textilmarkt

1958 TROPICAL MARKET
    f  Marché tropical
    d  Tropenmarkt

1959 CONQUEST OF MARKETS
    f  Conquête des marchés
    d  Erschliessung der Märkte

1960 DISLOCATION OF THE
    MARKET
    f  Dislocation du marché
    d  Auseinanderfallen des
       Marktes;
       Zersplitterung des
       Marktes

1961 LIMITATIONS OF THE
    MARKET
    f  Etroitesse du marché
    d  Enge des Marktes

1962 STRUCTURE OF THE
    MARKET
    f  Structure du marché
    d  Marktstruktur

1963 MARKETING
    f  Commercialisation;
       Marketing
    d  Kommerzialisierung;
       Vermarktung

1964 MARKETING ARRANGE-
    MENTS
    f  Accords de commercia-
       lisation
    d  Kommerzialisierungs-
       abkommen

1965 MARKETING BOARD
    f  Office de vente
    d  Kommerzialisierungs-
       büro

1966 MARKETING EXPERT
    f  Expert en commercia-
       lisation
    d  Marktexperte

1967 MARKETING RESEARCH
    f  Etude des marchés
    d  Marktforschung

1968 FOOD MARKETING
    f  Commercialisation des
       denrées alimentaires
    d  Kommerzialisierung der
       Lebensmittel

1969 HANDICRAFT MARKETING
    f  Commercialisation des
       produits de l'artisanat
    d  Kommerzialisierung
       kunsthandwerklicher
       Produkte

1970 LIVESTOCK MARKETING
    f  Commercialisation du
       bétail
    d  Kommerzialisierung
       der Viehzucht

102

1971 MERGER
  f Fusion
  d Zusammenschluss

1972 MOST-FAVOURED-NATION
  CLAUSE
  f Clause de la nation la
    plus favorisée
  d Meistbegünstigungs-
    klausel

1973 MOVEMENT OF FACTORS
  OF PRODUCTION
  f Circulation des facteurs
    de production
  d Freizügigkeit der
    Produktionsfaktoren

1974 CAPITAL MOVEMENT
  f Circulation du capital
  d Freizügigkeit des Kapi-
    tals;
    Kapitalfreizügigkeit

1975 COMMODITY MOVEMENTS;
  INTERFLOW OF GOODS
  f Circulation des
    marchandises;
    Circulation de biens
  d Freizügigkeit der Güter;
    Güterfreizügigkeit

1976 LABOUR MOVEMENT
  f Circulation de la main-
    d'oeuvre
  d Freizügigkeit der
    Arbeitskraft

1977 MULTILATERALISM
  f Multilatéralisme
  d Multilateralismus

1978 TARIFF NOMENCLATURE
  f Nomenclature douanière
  d Zolltarifschema

1979 BILATERAL ORGANIZATION
  f Organisation bilatérale
  d Bilaterale Organisation

1980 MULTILATERAL
  ORGANIZATION
  f Organisation multi-
    latérale
  d Multilaterale
    Organisation

1981 COUNTRY OF ORIGIN
  f Pays d'origine
  d Ursprungsland

1982 CERTIFICATE OF ORIGIN
  f Certificat d'origine
  d Ursprungszeugnis

1983 OUTLETS;
  MARKETS
  f Débouchés
  d Absatzgebiete

1984 OVERSEAS TERRITORIES
  f Territoires d'Outre-Mer
  d Überseegebiete

1985 PATTERN OF RETAIL
  SALES
  f Composition des ventes
    au détail
  d Struktur der Detail-
    verkäufe

1986 PEDDLER
  f Marchand ambulant
  d Ambulanter Verkäufer

1987 PREFERENTIAL RATE
  f Taux préférentiel
  d Präferenzzoll

1988 PREFERENTIAL SYSTEM;
  SYSTEM OF PREFERENCES
  f Système préférentiel;
    Système de préférences
  d Präferenzsystem

1989 PREFERENTIAL TARIFF
  f Tarif préférentiel
  d Präferenzzoll

1990 MARKET PRICE
  f Prix du marché
  d Marktpreis

104

2014 RESTRICTIVE MEASURES
 f Mesures restrictives
 d Restriktionsmassnahmen

2015 RETAILER
 f Détaillant
 d Detailhändler;
   Einzelhändler

2016 SALES REVENUES
 f Produit des ventes
 d Verkaufsertrag

2017 SALES TECHNICS
 f Techniques de vente
 d Verkaufstechniken

2018 SALES VOLUME;
 TURNOVER
 f Chiffre d'affaires
 d Umsatz

2019 AFTER SALE SERVICE
 f Service après-vente
 d Service nach Verkauf

2020 SATURATION POINT
 f Point de saturation
 d Sättigungspunkt

2021 SMALLNESS OF THE
 NATIONAL MARKET
 f Etroitesse du marché
   national
 d Enge des nationalen
   Marktes

2022 SMUGGLING;
 CONTREBANDE
 f Contrebande
 d Schmuggel

2023 SPECIAL REGULATIONS
 f Arrangements spéciaux
 d Sonderabkommen

2024 STATE INTERVENTION
 f Intervention de l'Etat
 d Staatliche Intervention

2025 STOCK EXCHANGE
 f Bourse (de valeurs)
 d (Wertpapier-)Börse

2026 INTERNATIONAL SUGAR
 CONFERENCE
 f Conférence internationale
   du sucre
 d Internationale Zucker-
   konferenz

2027 SUGAR MARKET
 f Marché sucrier
 d Zuckermarkt

2028 SUPPLIERS
 f Fournisseurs
 d Lieferanten

2029 SURPLUS PURCHASE
 f Achat d'excédents
 d Surpluskauf

2030 TARIFF BARRIERS
 f Barrières douanières
 d Zollschranken

2031 TARIFF POLICY
 f Politique douanière;
   Politique tarifaire
 d Zollpolitik

2032 TARIFF REDUCTION
 f Réduction de droits de
   douane
 d Zollreduktion

2033 PROTECTIVE TARIFFS;
 PROTECTIVE DUTIES
 f Droits protecteurs;
   Tarifs de protection
 d Schutzzölle

2034 ADJUSTMENT OF TARIFFS
 f Ajustement des tarifs
   douaniers
 d Angleichung der
   Schutzzölle

2035 AGREEMENT ON TARIFFS
 f Convention tarifaire
 d Zollabkommen

2036 UNIFICATION OF
TARIFFS
f  Unification des tarifs
douaniers
d  Vereinheitlichung der
Zölle

2037 TERMS OF TRADE
f  Termes de l'échange
d  Austauschbeziehungen

2038 TERMS OF TRADE EFFECTS
f  Effets sur les termes
de l'échange
d  "Terms of trade"-Effekte;
Auswirkungen der Aus-
tauschbeziehungen

2039 DETERIORATION IN
TERMS OF TRADE
f  Dégradation des termes
de l'échange
d  Verschlechterung der
"Terms of trade"

2040 TERRITORIAL IMBALANCE
f  Déséquilibre de l'espace
d  Territoriales Ungleich-
gewicht

2041 TONNAGE
f  Tonnage
d  Tonnage

2042 TRADE BARRIERS
f  Obstacles au commerce;
Entraves au commerce
d  Handelshindernisse

2043 "TRADE CREATION";
VINER, MEADE
f  Création de commerce
d  Handelsschaffung

2044 TRADE DEFICIT
f  Déficit commercial
d  Handelsdefizit

2045 TRADE EXHIBITION;
TRADE FAIR
f  Foire commerciale

d  Handelsausstellung;
Handelsmesse

2046 TRADE MARKETS
f  Marchés commerciaux
d  Handelsmärkte

2047 TRADE MISSIONS
f  Missions commerciales
d  Handelsmissionen

2048 TRADE PROMOTION AND
MARKETING
f  Développement du com-
merce et de la commer-
cialisation
d  Entwicklung des Handels
und der Kommerziali-
sierung

2049 TRADE RELATIONS
f  Relations commerciales
d  Handelsbeziehungen

2050 TRADE TRENDS
f  Orientation commerciale;
Orientation des échanges
d  Handelstendenzen;
Handelsorientierung

2051 TRADE AND DISTRIBUTION
f  Commerce et distribution
d  Handel und Verteilung

2052 BARTER TRADE
f  Troc
d  Kompensationshandel

2053 COMMODITIES TRADE
f  Commerce des produits
de base
d  Handel mit Basisprodukten

2054 DOMESTIC TRADE
f  Commerce intérieur
d  Lokaler Handel;
Binnenhandel

2055 EXPORT TRADE
f  Commerce d'exportation
d  Exporthandel

2056 EXTERNAL TRADE
    f  Commerce extérieur
    d  Aussenhandel

2057 FOREIGN TRADE IN
LIVE STOCK
    f  Commerce extérieur de
       bétail
    d  Viehaussenhandel

2058 INTRA-AREA TRADE
    f  Commerce à l'intérieur
       de la zone
    d  Interzonenhandel

2059 INVISIBLE TRADE
BALANCE
    f  Balance commerciale
       invisible
    d  Unsichtbare Handelsbilanz

2060 OVERALL TRADE
    f  Commerce d'ensemble
    d  Globalhandel

2061 RECIPROCAL TRADE
    f  Commerce réciproque
    d  Reziproker Handel

2062 RETAIL TRADE
    f  Commerce de détail
    d  Detailhandel;
       Kleinhandel

2063 TRANSIT TRADE
    f  Commerce de transit
    d  Transithandel

2064 VISIBLE TRADE BALANCE
    f  Balance commerciale
       visible
    d  Sichtbare Handelsbilanz

2065 CONCENTRATION OF
TRADE
    f  Centralisation du
       commerce
    d  Zentralisierung des
       Handels

2066 DEVELOPMENT OF TRADE
    f  Développement du
       commerce
    d  Handelsentwicklung

2067 INCREASE IN TRADE
    f  Accroissement des
       échanges
    d  Handelsexpansion

2068 PATTERN OF TRADE;
TRADE PATTERN
    f  Structure du commerce;
       Structure des échanges
    d  Handelsstruktur

2069 REFORMS IN TRADE
    f  Réformes commerciales
    d  Handelsreformen

2070 STABILITY OF TRADE
    f  Stabilité des échanges
    d  Stabilität der
       Handelsbeziehungen

2071 VOLUME OF TRADE
    f  Volume du trafic
       commercial
    d  Handelsvolumen

2072 VOLUME OF FOREIGN
TRADE
    f  Volume des échanges
       internationaux
    d  Volumen des Aussen-
       handels

2073 STATE TRADING
    f  Commerce d'Etat
    d  Staatlicher Handel

2074 STATE-TRADING
OPERATIONS
    f  Transaction relevant
       du commerce d'Etat
    d  Staatliche Handels-
       operationen

2075 STREET TRADING
    f  Vente ambulante
    d  Strassenhandel

2076 TRADING PERIOD
    f  Période de traite
    d  Handelsperiode

2077 TRADING PARTNER
    f  Partenaire commercial
    d  Handelspartner

2078 TRANSITIONAL PERIOD
    f  Période transitoire
    d  Übergangsperiode

2079 WORLD CONSUMPTION
    f  Consommation mondiale
    d  Weltkonsum

2080 WORLD MARKETS
    f  Marchés mondiaux
    d  Weltmärkte

2081 WORLD NEEDS
    f  Besoins mondiaux
    d  Weltbedarf

2082 WORLD ORGANIZATIONS
    f  Organisations internatio-
       nales;
       Organismes internationaux
    d  Weltorganisationen

2083 WORLD PRICES
    f  Prix mondiaux
    d  Weltmarktpreise

2084 WORLD PRODUCTION
    f  Production mondiale
    d  Weltproduktion

2085 WORLD TRADE
    f  Echanges mondiaux
    d  Welthandel

# IX.
## EDUCATION AND TRAINING
## EDUCATION ET FORMATION
## ERZIEHUNG UND AUSBILDUNG

2086 ACADEMIC AUTHORITIES
    f  Autorités académiques
    d  Akademische Behörden

2087 ACQUISITION OF SKILLS
    f  Spécialisation
    d  Spezialisierung

2088 ADVISER;
    COUNSELOR
    f  Conseiller
    d  Berater

2089 ADVISORY AID;
    CONSULTATIVE ASSIS-
    TANCE
    f  Aide consultative;
       Aide conseil
    d  Beratungshilfe

2090 APPRENTICESHIP
    SCHEMES
    f  Programmes d'appren-
       tissage
    d  Lehrlingsprogramme

2091 AUDIO-VISUAL AIDS
    f  Moyens audio-visuels
    d  Audio-visuelle Hilfen

2092 AUDIO-VISUAL MEANS
    f  Moyens audio-visuels
    d  Audio-visuelle Mittel

2093 BROADCASTING FOR
    THE MASS
    f  Radiodiffusion au service
       des masses
    d  Rundfunk für Massen-
       erziehung

2094 BUILDING UP NATIONAL
    MANPOWER
    f  Formation de ressources
       nationales de main-
       d'oeuvre
    d  Ausbildung von nationalen
       Arbeitskräften

2095 INDIGENOUS CADRE
    f  Cadres autochtones;
       Cadres nationaux
    d  Autochthoner Kader

2096 MIDDLE LEVEL CADRE
    f  Cadres moyens
    d  Mittlerer Kader

2097 AGRICULTURAL COLLEGE
    f  Ecole agricole
    d  Ackerbauschule

2098 VOCATIONAL COLLEGE
    f  Ecole professionnelle
    d  Berufsschule

2099 CONSULTATION GROUPS
    f  Groupes de consultation
    d  Beratungsgruppen

2100 CONSULTATIVE SERVICES
    f  Services consultatifs
    d  Beratungsdienste

2101 CONSULTING CENTRE
    f  Bureau de consultation
    d  Beratungsstelle

2102 CRAFTSMANSHIP
    f  Savoir faire artisanal;
       Habilité artisanale
    d  Handwerkliches Können

2103 CURRICULA
f Programme de l'enseignement
d Unterrichtsprogramm

2104 DEMONSTRATION
EQUIPMENT
f Matériel de démonstration
d Demonstrationsmaterial

2105 DIVERSIFICATION OF
SCHOOL CURRICULAE
f Diversification des
programmes d'études
d Diversifizierung der
Studienprogramme

2106 DROP-OUT-RATE
f Taux d'échec
d Ausfallsrate

2107 EDUCATION
f Enseignement
d Erziehungswesen

2108 EDUCATION OFFICER
f Administrateur de
l'enseignement
d Verwaltungsbeamter für
das Erziehungswesen

2109 EDUCATION SECTOR
f Secteur de l'enseignement
d Erziehungssektor

2110 EDUCATION SURVEY
f Etude du système scolaire
d Analyse des Schulsystems

2111 EDUCATION FOR
DEVELOPMENT
f Enseignement pour le
développement
d Erziehung für Entwicklung

2112 EDUCATION OF THE
MASSES;
MASS EDUCATION
f Education des masses;
Instruction des masses
d Massenerziehung

2113 AGRICULTURAL
EDUCATION
f Enseignement agricole
d Agrarerziehung

2114 AGRICULTURAL EDU-
CATION SPECIALIST
f Spécialiste de l'enseignement agricole
d Experte für Agrarer-
ziehung

2115 BASIC EDUCATION;
LITERACY
f Instruction élémentaire;
Education de base
d Grunderziehung

2116 COMMUNITY EDUCATION
f Education communautaire
d Kollektiverziehung

2117 "CONSUMER" EDUCATION
f Enseignement "Consom-
mation"
d Erziehung als "Konsum"

2118 CONTINUING EDUCATION
f Education continue
d Fortbildungswesen

2119 ELEMENTARY EDUCATION
f Enseignement élémentaire
d Elementare Erziehung

2120 FORMAL EDUCATION
f Instruction scolaire
d Schulausbildung

2121 FUNDAMENTAL EDUCATION
f Education de base
d Basiserziehung

2122 FUNCTIONAL TYPE OF
EDUCATION
f Enseignement rationnel
d Funktionelle Erziehung

2123 GENERAL EDUCATION
f Enseignement général
d Allgemeine Erziehung

2124 GIRL'S EDUCATION
   f   Education de la femme
   d   Erziehung der Frau

2125 HEALTH EDUCATION
   f   Education d'hygiène
   d   Gesundheitserziehung

2126 HIGHER EDUCATION
   f   Enseignement supérieur
   d   Höhere Erziehung

2127 INFORMAL EDUCATION
   f   Enseignement officieux
   d   Informelle Erziehung

2128 "INVESTMENT" EDUCATION
   f   Enseignement "Investisse-
      ment"
   d   Erziehung als "Investi-
      tion"

2129 LITERARY EDUCATION
   f   Enseignement littéraire
   d   Literarische Erziehung

2130 NATIONAL EDUCATION
   f   Education nationale
   d   Nationale Erziehung

2131 NOMAD EDUCATION
   f   Education des nomades
   d   Erziehung der Nomaden

2132 NON-SCHOLASTIC EDUCA-
     TION
   f   Enseignement non-scolaire
   d   Erziehung ausserhalb der
      Schule

2133 PRESCHOOL EDUCATION
   f   Enseignement préscolaire
   d   Erziehung vor dem
      Schulbesuch

2134 PRIMARY EDUCATION
   f   Enseignement primaire
   d   Primärerziehung

2135 PUBLIC EDUCATION
   f   Instruction publique;
      Enseignement publique
   d   Öffentliche Erziehung

2136 SCHOOL EDUCATION
   f   Enseignement scolaire
   d   Schulbildung

2137 SECONDARY EDUCATION
   f   Enseignement secondaire
   d   Sekundärerziehung

2138 STATE EDUCATION
   f   Education nationale
   d   Staatliche Erziehung

2139 TECHNICAL EDUCATION
   f   Enseignement technique
   d   Technische Erziehung

2140 UNIVERSITY EDUCATION
   f   Enseignement supérieur
   d   Universitätserziehung

2141 CONTENT OF EDUCATION
   f   Contenu de l'éducation
   d   Erziehungsinhalt

2142 DEVELOPMENT OF
     EDUCATION
   f   Développement de
      l'enseignement
   d   Erziehungsentwicklung

2143 ECONOMICS OF EDUCATION;
     EDUCATIONAL ECONOMICS
   f   Economie de l'éducation
   d   Bildungsökonomie

2144 LEVEL OF EDUCATION
   f   Degré d'instruction;
      Degré de l'enseignement
   d   Erziehungsniveau

2145 ORGANIZATION OF
     EDUCATION
   f   Organisation de l'en-
      seignement
   d   Erziehungsorganisation

2146 PURPOSE OF EDUCATION
   f   Objet de l'éducation
   d   Erziehungszweck

2147 SOCIOLOGY OF
EDUCATION
f  Sociologie de l'éducation
d  Erziehungssoziologie

2148 EDUCATIONAL
ADMINISTRATION
f  Administration des
établissements d'enseig-
nement
d  Verwaltung des
Erziehungswesens

2149 EDUCATIONAL
ADVANCEMENT
f  Amélioration de l'enseignement
d  Verbesserung des Er-
ziehungswesens

2150 EDUCATIONAL ASSISTANCE
f  Aide éducationnelle
d  Bildungshilfe

2151 EDUCATIONAL BROAD-
CASTING
f  Radio éducative;
Emission scolaire
d  Schulsendungen;
Radioerziehung

2152 EDUCATIONAL ESTABLISH-
MENT
f  Etablissement scolaire
d  Schulische Einrichtung

2153 EDUCATIONAL INFRA-
STRUCTURE
f  Infrastructure éducationnelle
d  Infrastruktur des
Erziehungswesens

2154 EDUCATIONAL LEVEL;
LEVEL OF EDUCATION
f  Niveau d'instruction
d  Erziehungsniveau

2155 EDUCATIONAL MISSION
f  Mission d'enseignement
d  Erziehungsmission

2156 EDUCATIONAL PLANNER
f  Planificateur de
l'éducation
d  Erziehungsplaner

2157 EDUCATIONAL PLANNING
f  Planification de l'enseignement;
Planification de l'éduca-
tion
d  Erziehungsplanung;
Bildungsplanung

2158 EDUCATIONAL PROGRAMME
f  Programme d'enseigne-
ment
d  Erziehungsprogramm

2159 EDUCATIONAL
PSYCHOLOGY
f  Psychologie pédagogique
d  Erziehungspsychologie

2160 EDUCATIONAL RESEARCH
f  Recherche pédagogique
d  Erziehungsforschung

2161 EDUCATIONAL REVOLU-
TION
f  Révolution d'enseignement
d  Erziehungsrevolution

2162 EDUCATIONAL STRUCTURE
f  Structure de l'enseignement
d  Erziehungsstruktur

2163 EDUCATIONAL TARGETS
f  Buts de l'enseignement
d  Erziehungsziele

2164 EDUCATIONAL TASKS
f  Tâches éducatives
d  Erziehungsaufgaben

2165 EDUCATIONAL TECHNOLO-
GY
f  Technologie de l'éducation
Technique pédagogique
d  Erziehungstechnologie;
Pädagogische Technik

2166 EDUCATIONAL WORK
    f  Oeuvre éducative
    d  Erziehungsarbeit

2167 HIGHER EDUCATIONAL
    INSTITUTIONS
    f  Etablissements d'enseig-
       nement supérieur
    d  Höhere Bildungsinstitu-
       tionen

2168 NATIONAL EDUCATIONAL
    SYSTEMS
    f  Systèmes d'enseignement
       nationaux
    d  Nationales Erziehungs-
       wesen

2169 ENROLEMENT RATIO
    f  Taux de scolarisation
    d  Beschulungsrate

2170 ENTRY STANDARDS
    f  Conditions d'admission
    d  Zulassungsbedingungen

2171 RECOGNITION OF
    DIPLOMAS
    f  Reconnaissance des
       diplômes
    d  Nostrifizierung von
       Diplomen

2172 EQUIVALENCY OF
    DIPLOMAS
    f  Equivalence des diplômes
    d  Gleichwertigkeit der
       Diplome

2173 MANUAL EXPERIENCE
    f  Expérience manuelle
    d  Manuelle Erfahrung

2174 PRACTICAL EXPERIENCE
    f  Expérience pratique
    d  Praktische Erfahrung

2175 EXPERIMENTAL STATION
    f  Station expérimentale
    d  Versuchsstation

2176 EXPERT
    f  Expert;
       Spécialiste
    d  Experte

2177 POOL OF EXPERTS
    f  Corps d'experts;
       Equipe d'experts
    d  Expertencorps

2178 EXTENSION OF PRIMARY
    EDUCATION
    f  Généralisation de
       l'enseignement primaire
    d  Verbreitung der
       Primärerziehung

2179 LOCAL FACILITIES
    f  Moyens locaux
    d  Lokale Mittel

2180 FILM LIBRARY
    f  Cinéthèque
    d  Filmbibliothek

2181 FOREST FORMATION
    f  Formation forestière
    d  Forstwirtschaftliche
       Ausbildung

2182 FORMING OF LABOURERS
    f  Formation des travailleurs
    d  Ausbildung von Arbeitern

2183 HUMAN CAPITAL
    f  Capital humain
    d  "Human Capital";
       "Menschliches Kapital"

2184 HUMAN FACTOR
    f  Facteur humain
    d  Menschlicher Faktor

2185 HUMAN INVESTMENT
    f  Investissement humain
    d  "Human Investment"

2186 HUMAN RESOURCES
    f  Ressources humaines;
       Potentiel humain
    d  Menschliche Reserven

2187 HUMANITIES
   f  Etudes classiques;
     Humanités
   d  Humanistische Erziehung

2188 ILLITERACY
   f  Analphabétisme
   d  Analphabetismus

2189 IMPROVEMENT IN EDU-
     CATIONAL FACILITIES
   f  Progrès des moyens
     d'enseignement
   d  Verbesserung der
     Erziehungsmittel

2190 IMPROVEMENT OF
     MANPOWER
   f  Perfectionnement de la
     main-d'oeuvre
   d  Verbesserung der
     Arbeitskraft

2191 IN-SERVICE
   f  Stage
   d  Praktikum

2192 INSTITUTE OF HIGHER
     LEARNING
   f  Institut d'enseignement
     supérieur
   d  Institut für höhere
     Erziehung

2193 TECHNICAL INSTITUTE
   f  Institut technique
   d  Technisches Institut

2194 TECHNICAL TRAINING
     INSTITUTE
   f  Institut de formation
     technique
   d  Institut für technische
     Ausbildung

2195 INSTITUTIONS OF HIGHER
     EDUCATION
   f  Institutions d'enseigne-
     ment supérieur
   d  Höhere Lehranstalten

2196 EDUCATIONAL
     INSTITUTIONS
   f  Institutions éducatives
   d  Erziehungsinstitute

2197 LOCAL INSTITUTIONS
   f  Etablissements locaux
   d  Lokale Institutionen

2198 ADDITIONAL INSTRUCTION
   f  Instruction complémen-
     taire
   d  Komplementäre Aus-
     bildung

2199 TECHNICAL INSTRUCTION
   f  Enseignement technique
   d  Technische Ausbildung

2200 INSTRUCTOR
   f  Moniteur;
     Instructeur
   d  Ausbildner

2201 INVENTORY OF TRAINING
     FACILITIES
   f  Inventaire des moyens
     de formation
   d  Inventar der Ausbildungs-
     möglichkeiten

2202 LACK OF COMPETENCE
   f  Manque de compétence
   d  Kompetenzmangel

2203 LANGUAGE PROBLEMS
   f  Problèmes linguistiques
   d  Sprachprobleme

2204 PROGRAMMED LEARNING
   f  Instruction programmée
   d  Programmierte Aus-
     bildung

2205 CAPACITY OF LEARNING
   f  Capacité d'absorption
   d  Aufnahmefähigkeit

2206 LITERACY CAMPAIGN
   f  Campagne d'alphabéti-
     sation
   d  Alphabetisierungs-
     kampagne

207 ADULT LITERACY
   f  Alphabétisation des
      adultes
   d  Erwachsenen-Alpha-
      betisierung

208 LOCATION OF TRAINING
   f  Localisation de centres
      de formation
   d  Lokalisierung der
      Ausbildung

209 MANAGEMENT DEVELOP-
    MENT
   f  Perfectionnement des
      cadres
   d  Entwicklung der Kader

210 MANAGEMENT TECHNIQUES
   f  Techniques de gestion
   d  Managementtechniken

211 MASS COMMUNICATION
   f  Moyen de communication
      de masse
   d  Massenkommunikation

212 MOBILIZATION OF HUMAN
    RESOURCES
   f  Mobilisation des res-
      sources humaines
   d  Mobilisierung von
      menschlichen Reserven

213 RURAL NEWSPAPERS
   f  Journaux ruraux
   d  Zeitungen für ländliche
      Gebiete

214 OCCUPATIONAL CHOICE
   f  Choix d'une profession
   d  Berufswahl

215 OFFICE FOR TECHNICAL
    TRAINING
   f  Bureau de la formation
      technique
   d  Zentrum für technische
      Ausbildung

2216 ORDER OF TRAINING
     PRIORITIES
    f  Ordre de priorité de
       la formation
    d  Prioritätsordnung der
       Ausbildung

2217 ORIENTATION COURSE
    f  Cours d'orientation
    d  Orientierungskurs

2218 ORIENTATION CYCLE
    f  Cycle d'orientation
    d  Orientierungszyklus

2219 OVERPRODUCTION OF
     CERTAIN CATEGORIES
     OF TRAINED PERSONNEL
    f  Surproduction de cer-
       taines catégories de
       personnel qualifié
    d  Überproduktion bestimmter
       Berufsgruppen

2220 EXPATRIATE PERSONNEL
    f  Personnel étranger;
       Personnel expatrié
    d  Ausländisches Personal

2221 HEALTH PERSONNEL
    f  Personnel d'hygiène
       publique
    d  Personal für das
       Gesundheitswesen

2222 SCIENTIFIC PERSONNEL
    f  Personnel scientifique
    d  Wissenschaftliches
       Personal

2223 TOP PERSONNEL
    f  Cadres supérieurs
    d  Hoher Kader

2224 PERSONS ABOVE SCHOOL
     AGE
    f  Population post-scolaire
    d  Bevölkerung nach dem
       Beschulungsalter

2225 PERSONS TRAINED
ABROAD
f  Personnel de formation
à l'étranger
d  Im Ausland ausgebildetes
Personal

2226 PILOT FARM
f  Ferme pilote
d  Musterfarm

2227 PILOT SCHOOL
f  Ecole pilote
d  Musterschule

2228 PIONEER DISTRICT
f  Secteur pilote
d  Versuchsbezirk

2229 PLANNING OF SCHOOL
ENROLEMENT
f  Planification de la
scolarisation
d  Skolarisationsplanung;
Beschulungsplanung

2230 POPULATION ATTENDING
SCHOOL
f  Population scolarisée
d  Beschulter Bevölkerungsteil

2231 POST-GRADUATE STUDIES
f  Etudes post-universitaires
d  Postgraduierte Studien

2232 RECRUITMENT PROCE-
DURES
f  Procédures de recrute-
ment
d  Rekrutierungsverfahren

2233 METHODS OF RECRUIT-
MENT
f  Procédés de recrutement
d  Rekrutierungsmethoden

2234 REFRESHER COURSE
f  Cours d'entretien
d  Auffrischungskurs

2235 REPAIR SHOP
f  Atelier de réparation
d  Werkstätte

2236 FOREIGN SCHOLARSHIPS
f  Bourses pour des études
à l'étranger
d  Stipendien für Auslands-
studien

2237 GOVERNMENT SCHOLAR-
SHIPS
f  Bourses du gouvernement
d  Regierungsstipendien

2238 GRADUATE SCHOLARSHIP;
EXTENSION SCHOLARSHIP
f  Extension perfectionnement;
Bourse de perfectionne-
ment
d  Weiterbildungsstipendien

2239 SCHOOL ATTENDANCE
f  Fréquentation scolaire
d  Schulbesuch

2240 SCHOOL FEEDING
f  Alimentation à l'école;
Repas scolaires
d  Schulausspeisung

2241 SCHOOL LEAVERS
f  Elèves en fin de scolarité
d  Schulabsolventen

2242 BUSH SCHOOL
f  Ecole de brousse
d  Schule im Busch

2243 BUSINESS SCHOOLS
f  Ecoles commerciales
d  Handelsschulen

2244 GOVERNMENT SCHOOL
f  Ecole gouvernementale
d  Staatliche Schule

2245 TECHNICAL SCHOOL
f  Ecole technique
d  Technische Schule

2246 SHORTAGE OF TEACHERS
f Pénurie d'instituteurs
d Lehrermangel

2247 SHORTAGE OF SENIOR
PERSONNEL
f Pénuries de cadres
d Mangel an Kadern

2248 SHORTAGE OF TECHNICAL
PERSONNEL
f Pénurie de personnel
technique
d Mangel an technischem
Personal

2249 SHORTFALL IN SKILLS
f Pénurie de compétences
d Mangel an Fachkräften

2250 STAFF DEVELOPMENT
CENTRE
f Centre de formation de
cadres
d Zentrum zur Kaderaus-
bildung

2251 STAFF REQUIREMENTS
f Besoins en personnel
d Personalerfordernisse

2252 SENIOR STAFF;
EXECUTIVE STAFF
f Cadres supérieurs;
Personnel supérieur
d Leitendes Personal

2253 STUDENT ASSOCIATIONS
f Associations d'étudiants
d Studentenorganisationen

2254 STUDENT POPULATION
f Population scolaire
d Schüleranzahl

2255 STUDENT REPRESENTA-
TION
f Représentation d'étudiants
d Studentische Vertretung

2256 STUDY TOURS
f Voyages d'études
d Studienreise

2257 SUPERVISOR
f Moniteur-inspecteur
d Praktikumsleiter

2258 TEACHING AIDS;
COURSE MATERIALS
f Matériel d'enseignement
d Unterrichtsmaterial

2259 TEACHING CENTRE;
TEACHING ESTABLISH-
MENT
f Centre d'enseignement
d Unterrichtszentrum

2260 TEACHING EQUIPMENT
f Matériel pédagogique
d Pädagogisches Material

2261 TEACHING TECHNIQUES
f Techniques pédagogiques
d Pädagogische Techniken

2262 TEACHER TRAINING
f Formation pédagogique;
Enseignement normal
d Pädagogische Ausbildung

2263 TEACHER TRAINING
CENTER
f Centre d'enseignement
normal
d Lehrerausbildungsanstalt

2264 INDUSTRIAL TEACHER
TRAINING
f Formation des institu-
teurs industriels
d Ausbildung von industriel-
lem Lehrpersonal

2265 RURAL TEACHER
TRAINING
f Formation des institu-
teurs ruraux
d Ausbildung von land-
wirtschaftlichem Lehr-
personal

2266 MULTI-PURPOSE TEAM
    f   Equipe polyvalente
    d   Mehrzweckteam

2267 TEAM LEADER
    f   Chef d'équipe;
       Chef de groupe
    d   Teamführer;
       Gruppenführer

2268 UNCERTIFIED TEACHER
    f   Instituteur non-diplômé
    d   Undiplomierter Lehrer

2269 TECHNICAL COLLEGE;
     TECHNICAL HIGH SCHOOL
    f   Ecole technique
    d   Technikum;
       Technische Mittelschule

2270 TECHNICAL PERSONNEL
    f   Techniciens
    d   Techniker

2271 TECHNICAL PERSONNEL
     TRAINING
    f   Formation de personnel
       technique
    d   Ausbildung von tech-
       nischem Personal

2272 TRAINEE
    f   Stagiaire
    d   Praktikant

2273 GOVERNMENT SPONSOR
     TRAINEE;
     GOVERNMENT SUPPORTED
     TRAINEE
    f   Stagiaire de l'Etat
    d   Regierungspraktikant

2274 TRAINING ACTIVITIES
    f   Activités de formation
    d   Ausbildungstätigkeit

2275 TRAINING ASSISTANCE
    f   Aide à la formation
       professionnelle
    d   Ausbildungshilfe

2276 TRAINING CENTRE
    f   Centre de formation
    d   Ausbildungsstätte

2277 TRAINING COORDINATION
    f   Coordination de la
       formation
    d   Koordinierung der
       Ausbildung

2278 TRAINING COURSE
    f   Stage
    d   Ausbildungskurs

2279 TRAINING FACILITIES
    f   Moyens de formation
    d   Ausbildungsmöglich-
       keiten

2280 TRAINING FARM;
     AGRICULTURAL TRAINING
     CENTRE
    f   Ferme-école;
       Ferme d'apprentissage
    d   Landwirtschaftlicher
       Lehrbetrieb

2281 TRAINING MACHINERY
    f   Système de formation
    d   Ausbildungssystem

2282 TRAINING METHOD
    f   Méthode de formation
    d   Ausbildungsmethode

2283 TRAINING OFFICER
    f   Chargé de la formation
    d   Ausbildungsbeamter

2284 TRAINING POLICY
    f   Politique de formation
    d   Ausbildungspolitik

2285 TRAINING PRIORITIES
    f   Priorités de la formation
    d   Ausbildungsprioritäten

2286 TRAINING PROGRAMME
    f   Programme de formation
    d   Ausbildungsprogramm

2287 TRAINING PROMOTION
    f  Promotion de la formation
    d  Förderung der Ausbildung

2288 TRAINING REQUIREMENTS
    f  Besoins en matière de
       formation
    d  Ausbildungsbedarf

2289 TRAINING STRATEGY
    f  Stratégie de la formation
    d  Ausbildungsstrategie

2290 ADVANCED TRAINING
    f  Formation supérieure
    d  Höhere Ausbildung

2291 ACCELERATED TRAINING
    f  Formation accélérée
    d  Kurzausbildung

2292 BASIC TRAINING;
     PRELIMINARY TRAINING
    f  Formation préliminaire
    d  Vorausbildung

2293 BASIC TRAINING
    f  Formation de base
    d  Grundausbildung

2294 CIVIL SERVICE TRAINING
    f  Formation de la fonction
       publique
    d  Ausbildung von Staats-
       beamten

2295 CLERICAL TRAINING
    f  Formation des employés
    d  Ausbildung von Ange-
       stellten

2296 FARMER TRAINING
    f  Education des cultivateurs
    d  Ausbildung von Landwirten

2297 FOREMAN-TRAINEE
    f  Centremaître stagiaire
    d  Ausbildung von Vor-
       arbeitern

2298 HEAD OF TRAINING
    f  Chef de la division
       formation
    d  Ausbildungsleiter

2299 LABOUR TRAINING
    f  Formation de la
       main-d'oeuvre
    d  Ausbildung der Arbeits-
       kraft

2300 MANUAL TRAINING
    f  Formation des travailleurs
       manuels
    d  Ausbildung von manuellen
       Arbeitskräften

2301 ON-THE-JOB TRAINING
    f  Formation sur le tas;
       Formation en cours
       d'emplois
    d  Ausbildung auf dem
       Arbeitsplatz

2302 OVERSEAS TRAINING;
     TRAINING ABROAD
    f  Formation à l'étranger;
       Etudes à l'étranger
    d  Auslandsausbildung

2303 PLANNED TRAINING
    f  Formation planifiée
    d  Geplante Ausbildung

2304 POPULAR TRAINING
     CENTRE
    f  Centre populaire de
       formation
    d  Ausbildungszentren für
       die gesamte Bevölkerung

2305 PRACTICAL TRAINING
    f  Formation pratique
    d  Praktische Ausbildung

2306 PREVOCATIONAL
     TRAINING
    f  Enseignement pré-pro-
       fessionnel
    d  Vorprofessionnelle
       Erziehung

2307 RETRAINING
   f  Ré-éducation
   d  Umerziehung

2308 THEORETICAL TRAINING
   f  Formation théorique
   d  Theoretische Ausbildung

2309 TYPE OF TRAINING
   f  Type de formation
   d  Ausbildungsart

2310 TRAINING OF CADRES;
   MANAGEMENT TRAINING
   f  Formation des cadres
   d  Ausbildung von Kadern

2311 TRAINING OF FUTURE
   STAFF;
   TRAINING OF YOUNG
   PEOPLE
   f  Formation des jeunes
   d  Nachwuchsförderung

2312 TRAINING OF TECHNICIANS
   f  Formation de techniciens
   d  Ausbildung von Technikern

2313 TRANSFER OF KNOWLEDGE
   f  Transfert de connaissance
   d  Wissensvermittlung

2314 UNIVERSITY EXTENSION
   f  Extension universitaire
   d  Volkshochschule

2315 UNIVERSITY MEN
   f  Universitaires
   d  Universitätsabsolventen

2316 UNIVERSITY STUDIES
   f  Etudes universitaires
   d  Universitätsstudien

2317 VOCATIONAL GUIDANCE
   f  Orientation professionnelle
   d  Berufsorientierung;
   Berufsberatung

2318 VOCATIONAL GUIDANCE
   CENTRE
   f  Centre d'orientation
   professionnelle
   d  Berufsberatungsstelle

2319 VOCATIONAL SKILL
   f  Compétences profession-
   nelles
   d  Berufskompetenz

2320 VOCATIONAL TRAINING
   f  Formation professionnelle
   d  Berufsausbildung

2321 VOCATIONAL TRAINING
   CENTRES
   f  Centres de formation
   d  Fachliche Ausbildungs-
   stätten

2322 WASTE
   f  Gaspillage
   d  Schulungsverluste

2323 INTELLECTUAL WASTAGE
   f  Gaspillage intellectuel
   d  Intellektuelle Vergeudung

2324 WORKSHOP PRACTICE
   f  Travail d'atelier
   d  Werkstättenerfahrung

2325 JOINT WORKSHOP
   f  Atelier d'apprentissage
   en commun
   d  Lehrwerkstättenzentrum

2326 PILOT WORKSHOP
   f  Atelier pilote
   d  Musterwerkstätte

# X.

## POPULATION AND MANPOWER
## POPULATION ET MAIN-D'OEUVRE
## BEVÖLKERUNG UND ARBEITSKRAFT

2327 ABSENTEEISM
    f  Absentéisme
    d  Arbeitsversäumnis

2328 AGE COMPOSITION
    f  Composition par groupe
       d'âge
    d  Alterszusammensetzung

2329 AGE OF DEPENDENCY
    f  Age non-productif
    d  Unproduktives Alter

2330 AGE PYRAMID
    f  Pyramide des âges
    d  Alterspyramide

2331 AGE STRUCTURE
    f  Structure par âge
    d  Altersstruktur

2332 BEHAVIOUR PATTERN
    f  Formes de comportement
    d  Verhaltensgefüge

2333 BIRTH CONTROL
    f  Contrôle des naissances
    d  Geburtenkontrolle

2334 HIGH BIRTH RATE
    f  Taux démographique
       élevé
    d  Hohe Geburtsrate

2335 NUMBER OF LIVE BIRTHS
    f  Nombre de naissances
       vivantes
    d  Anzahl der Lebendge-
       burten

2336 CENSUS AREA
    f  Territoire de recensement
    d  Gebiet einer Volkszählung

2337 RETURNS OF A CENSUS
    f  Résultats d'un recense-
       ment
    d  Resultat einer Volks-
       zählung

2338 CIVIL SERVANTS
    f  Fonctionnaires
    d  Beamtenschaft

2339 DOMINANT CLASS
    f  Classe exploitante
    d  Dominierende Klasse

2340 WORKING CLASS
    f  Classe ouvrière
    d  Arbeiterklasse

2341 COLONIES WITH LARGE
    WHITE MINORITIES
    f  Colonies avec de fortes
       minorités blanches
    d  Bevölkerungskolonien

2342 COMMUNITY ACTIVITIES
    f  Activités communautaires
    d  Kollektivtätigkeiten

2343 COMMUNITY CENTRE
    f  Centre social
    d  Soziales Zentrum

2344 COMMUNITY FACILITIES
    f  Installations collectives
    d  Kollektiveinrichtungen

2345 COMMUNITY SERVICE
    f  Service social des
       collectivités
    d  Kollektivdienst

2346 COMPOSITION OF A
POPULATION
f Structure d'une population
d Bevölkerungsstruktur

2347 AGE AND SEX COMPOSITION
f Réparition par âge et sexe
d Bevölkerungsstruktur nach
Alter und Geschlecht

2348 COOPERATIVE MOVEMENT
f Mouvement coopératif
d Genossenschaftsbewegung

2349 FORMS OF COOPERATIVES
f Formes de coopératives
d Genossenschaftsformen

2350 COST OF LIVING
f Coût de la vie
d Lebenskosten

2351 LOCAL COUNTER-PART
f Technicien local
d Lokaler Techniker

2352 CULTURAL COOPERATION
f Collaboration culturelle
d Kulturelle Zusammen-
arbeit

2353 DEMO-ECONOMIC
CHARACTERISTICS
f Caractéristiques
démo-économiques
d Demo-ökonomische
Faktoren

2354 DEMOGRAPHIC INDICATORS
f Indicateurs démographi-
ques
d Demographische Indika-
toren

2355 DEMOGRAPHIC INCREASE
f Accroissement démo-
graphique
d Demographische Zunahme

2356 DEMOGRAPHIC PRESSURE
f Pression démographique
d Bevölkerungsdruck

2357 DEMOGRAPHIC PROBLEMS
f Problèmes démographiques
d Demographische Probleme

2358 DEMOGRAPHIC SITUATION
f Situation démographique
d Demographische Situ-
ation

2359 DEMOGRAPHICAL ASPECTS
f Aspects démographiques
d Demographische Aspekte

2360 DEMOGRAPHY
f Démographie
d Demographie

2361 DEVELOPMENT OF HUMAN
RESOURCES
f Mise en valeur des
ressources humaines
d Entwicklung menschlicher
Reserven

2362 HEALTH DEVELOPMENT
f Développement d'hygiène
publique
d Entwicklung sanitärer
Projekte

2363 URBAN DEVELOPMENT
f Aménagement des
agglomérations
d Urbane Entwicklung

2364 DWELLINGS
f Habitations
d Wohnungen

2365 EMPLOYMENT CREATING
f Création d'emplois
d Schaffung von Arbeits-
plätzen

2366 EMPLOYMENT POLICY
f Politique en matière
d'emploi
d Beschäftigungspolitik

2367 EMPLOYMENT POTENTIAL
f Potentiel d'emploi
d Potentielle Beschäftigung

2368 FULL EMPLOYMENT
POLICY
f Politique de plein emploi
d Vollbeschäftigungspolitik

2369 GAINFUL EMPLOYMENT
f Emploi rémunérateur
d Remunerative Beschäfti-
gung

2370 PLACE OF EMPLOYMENT
f Lieu d'emploi
d Beschäftigungsstelle

2371 REALISTIC EMPLOYMENT
OPPORTUNITIES
f Possibilités d'emploi
objectives
d Beschäftigungsmöglich-
keit

2372 WAGE EMPLOYMENT
f Emploi rémunéré
d Bezahlte Beschäftigung;
Beschäftigung gegen
Entgelt

2373 AUTOCHTHON EXPERTS
f Spécialistes d'origine
indigène
d Fachleute aus der ein-
geborenen Bevölkerung;
Einheimische Fachleute

2374 FOREIGN EXPERT
f Expert étranger
d Ausländischer Experte

2375 LEGAL EXPERT
f Expert juridique
d Juristische Fachkraft

2376 FAMILY INCOME
f Revenu familial
d Familieneinkommen

2377 FAMILY LIMITATION
f Restriction volontaire
des naissances;
Limitation des naissances
d Geburtenbeschränkung

2378 FAMILY PLANNING
f Planning familial;
Planification familiale
d Familienplanung

2379 FAMILY WELFARE
MEASURES
f Prévoyance familiale
d Familienförderungsmass-
nahmen

2380 COMPOSITION OF THE
FAMILY
f Composition familiale
d Familiengrösse

2381 FERTILITY INDEX
f Indice de fécondité
d Fruchtbarkeitsindex

2382 FERTILITY RATE
f Taux de fécondité
d Fruchtbarkeitsrate

2383 FOOD AND DIETETICS
f Hygiène de l'alimentation
d Ernährungshygiene

2384 FOOD POLICY
f Politique alimentaire
d Ernährungspolitik

2385 SHORTAGE OF FOOD
f Pénurie de produits
alimentaires
d Nahrungsmangel

2386 FREEDOM OF MOVEMENT
f Circulation des
travailleurs
d Freizügigkeit der
Arbeitskraft

2387 HUMAN RESOURCES
PLANNING
f Planification des
ressources humaines
d Planung menschlicher
Reserven

2388 IMMIGRATION QUOTA
    f  Contingent d'immigration;
      Quota d'immigration
    d  Einwanderungskontingent

2389 RELATIVE INCOMES
    f  Revenus proportionnels
    d  Einkommensverhältnisse

2390 INFANT MORTALITY
    f  Mortalité infantile
    d  Kindersterblichkeit

2391 JOB ATTITUDE
    f  Comportement profes-
      sionnel
    d  Verhalten am Arbeits-
      platz

2392 JOB DESCRIPTION
    f  Spécification du travail;
      Description de poste
    d  Tätigkeitsbeschreibung

2393 JOB EVALUATION
    f  Qualification du travail;
      Qualification des postes
      de travail
    d  Arbeitsplatzbewertung

2394 JOB SEEKERS
    f  Chômeurs
    d  Arbeitslose

2395 AVAILABLE JOB
    f  Emploi disponible
    d  Vakanter Arbeitsplatz

2396 FULL-TIME JOB
    f  Emploi à plein temps
    d  Ganztagsarbeit

2397 NUMBER OF JOBS CREATED
    f  Nombre d'emplois
      créés
    d  Anzahl der neuen Arbeits-
      plätze

2398 PART-TIME JOB
    f  Emploi à mi-temps
    d  Halbtagsarbeit

2399 JUVENILE DELINQUENCY
    f  Délinquance juvénile
    d  Jugendkriminalität

2400 LABOUR CONTRACT
    f  Contrat de travail
    d  Arbeitsvertrag

2401 LABOUR COST
    f  Coût en main-d'oeuvre
    d  Arbeitskosten

2402 LABOUR ECONOMICS
    f  Economie du travail
    d  Ökonomie der Arbeits-
      kraft

2403 LABOUR EMPLOYMENT
    OFFICE
    f  Service de placement
    d  Büro für Arbeitsver-
      mittlung

2404 LABOUR LEGISLATION
    f  Législation du travail
    d  Arbeitsgesetzgebung

2405 LABOUR MARKET
    f  Marché du travail
    d  Arbeitsmarkt

2406 LABOUR METHODS
    f  Méthodes de travail
    d  Arbeitsmethoden

2407 LABOUR MOBILITY
    f  Mobilité de la main-
      d'oeuvre
    d  Arbeitsmobilität

2408 LABOUR POTENTIAL
    f  Potentiel en main-
      d'oeuvre
    d  Arbeitskräftepotential

2409 LABOUR PRODUCTIVITY
    f  Productivité du travail
    d  Arbeitsproduktivität

2410 LABOUR PROBLEMS
    f  Problèmes du travail
    d  Arbeitsprobleme

2411  LABOUR SERVICE
    f  Service de travail
    d  Arbeitsdienst

2412  LABOUR TURNOVER
    f  Instabilité de la
       main-d'oeuvre
    d  Instabilität der
       Arbeitskraft

2413  LABOUR VALUE
    f  Valeur travail
    d  Arbeitswert

2414  LABOUR UNIONS;
      TRADE UNIONS
    f  Syndicats
    d  Gewerkschaften

2415  COMPULSORY LABOUR;
      FORCED LABOUR
    f  Travail forcé;
       Travail obligatoire
    d  Zwangsarbeit

2416  FOREIGN LABOUR
    f  Main-d'oeuvre étrangère
    d  Ausländische Arbeits-
       kraft

2417  INTELLECTUAL LABOUR
    f  Travail intellectuel
    d  Geistige Arbeit

2418  LOCAL LABOUR
    f  Travail local
    d  Lokale Arbeitskraft

2419  MANUAL LABOUR
    f  Travail manuel
    d  Manuelle Arbeitskraft

2420  MOBILIZATION OF
      LABOUR
    f  Mobilisation du travail
    d  Arbeitsmobilisierung

2421  NATIVE LABOUR FORCE
    f  Main-d'oeuvre indigène
    d  Lokale Arbeitskraft

2422  LABOUR ORGANIZATIONS
    f  Organisations de travail
    d  Arbeitsorganisationen

2423  SKILLED LABOUR
    f  Main-d'oeuvre qualifiée;
       Ouvriers qualifiés;
       Ouvriers spécialisés
    d  Facharbeiter

2424  VOLUNTARY LABOUR
    f  Travail volontaire
    d  Arbeit auf freiwilliger
       Basis;
       Freiwilliger Arbeits-
       einsatz

2425  NEW ENTRIES INTO THE
      LABOUR FORCE
    f  Chiffre des entrées sur
       le marché du travail
    d  Neueintritte in den
       Arbeitsmarkt

2426  SOCIOLOGY OF LABOUR
    f  Sociologie du travail
    d  Arbeitssoziologie

2427  SUBSISTENCE THEORY OF
      LABOUR SUPPLY
    f  Loi d'airain des salaires
    d  Ehernes Lohngesetz

2428  LABOUR LEGISLATION
    f  Législation du travail
    d  Arbeitsgesetzgebung

2429  SOCIAL LEGISLATION
    f  Législation sociale
    d  Sozialgesetzgebung

2430  LEPROSARIUM
    f  Léprosarium
    d  Leprastation

2431  LEPROSY;
      LEPERS
    f  Lèpre
    d  Lepra

126

2432 MALARIA CONTROL
  f Lutte contre le paludisme
  d Malariakontrolle

2433 EXECUTIVE MANAGERS
  f Dirigeants exécutifs
  d Ausführender Kader

2434 MAN-LAND RATIO
  f Densité de la population
  d Besiedlungsdichte

2435 MANPOWER ASSESSMENT
  f Evaluation de la main-
    d'oeuvre
  d Beurteilung der Arbeits-
    kräfte

2436 MANPOWER BUDGETING
  f Prévisions budgétaires
    à l'égard de la main-
    d'oeuvre
  d Budgetvoranschlag für
    Arbeitskräfte

2437 MANPOWER EXPORTS
  f Exportations de main-
    d'oeuvre
  d Arbeitskräfteexport

2438 MANPOWER NEEDS
  f Besoins en main-d'oeuvre
  d Arbeitskräftebedarf

2439 MANPOWER ORGANIZATION
  f Organisation de la main-
    d'oeuvre
  d Organisation der Arbeits-
    kraft

2440 MANPOWER PLANNING;
  LABOUR FORCE PLANNING
  f Planification de la main-
    d'oeuvre
  d Arbeitskräfteplanung;
    Planung der Arbeits-
    kräfte

2441 MANPOWER PLANNING
  AUTHORITY
  f Service de planification
    de la main-d'oeuvre

  d Planungsbehörde für
    Arbeitskräfte

2442 MANPOWER PROBLEMS
  f Problèmes de main-
    d'oeuvre
  d Arbeitskräfteprobleme

2443 MANPOWER PROGRAM-
  MING TECHNIQUES
  f Techniques de programma-
    tion de la main-d'oeuvre
  d Techniken der Arbeits-
    kraftprogrammierung

2444 MANPOWER PYRAMID
  f Pyramide de la main-
    d'oeuvre
  d Pyramide der Arbeits-
    kräfte

2445 MANPOWER RESOURCES
  f Ressources en main-
    d'oeuvre
  d Arbeitskräftereserven

2446 MANPOWER SHORTAGE;
  SHORTAGE OF HANDICRAFT
  f Pénurie de main-d'oeuvre
  d Mangel an Arbeitskräften

2447 MANPOWER SITUATION
  f Situation de la main-
    d'oeuvre
  d Situation der Arbeitskraft

2448 MANPOWER SURVEY
  f Enquête sur la main-
    d'oeuvre
  d Arbeitskrafterhebung

2449 MANPOWER TRENDS
  f Tendance de la main-
    d'oeuvre
  d Tendenz der Arbeitskraft

2450 POTENTIAL MANPOWER
  f Ressources potentielles
    en main-d'oeuvre;
    Main-d'oeuvre potentielle
  d Potentielle Arbeitskräfte-
    reserven;
    Potentielle Arbeitskraft

2451 PROSPECTIVE MANPOWER
    f   Main-d'oeuvre future
    d   Zukünftige Arbeitskraft

2452 REGIONAL MANPOWER
    ADVISER
    f   Conseiller régional en
       main-d'oeuvre
    d   Regionalberater für
       Arbeitskräfte

2453 SHORTAGE OF SPECIA-
    LIZED MANPOWER
    f   Pénurie de main-d'oeuvre
       spécialisée
    d   Mangel an Facharbeitern

2454 STABILIZATION OF
    MANPOWER
    f   Stabilisation de la
       main-d'oeuvre
    d   Stabilisierung der
       Arbeitskraft

2455 MEDICAL AID;
    MEDICAL ASSISTANCE
    f   Assistance médicale
    d   Medizinische Hilfe

2456 MEDICAL SERVICES
    f   Infrastructure médicale
    d   Medizinische Dienste

2457 PREVENTIVE MEDICINE
    f   Médicine préventive
    d   Präventivmedizin

2458 TROPICAL MEDICINE
    f   Médicine tropicale
    d   Tropenmedizin

2459 MIDDLE CLASS
    f   Classes moyennes
    d   Mittelklasse

2460 MIGRATION
    f   Exode rural;
       Migration
    d   Landflucht

2461 INTERNAL MIGRATION
    f   Migration interne
    d   Interne Wanderbewegung

2462 INTERNATIONAL
    MIGRATION
    f   Migration internationale
    d   Internationale Wander-
       bewegung

2463 OVERSEAS MIGRATION
    f   Migration d'Outre-Mer
    d   Übersee-Auswanderung

2464 PATTERN OF MIGRATION
    f   Structure de migration
    d   Struktur der Wanderung

2465 SEASONAL MIGRATION
    f   Déplacement saisonnier
    d   Saisonale Wanderung

2466 FEMININE MILITANCY
    f   Animation féminine
    d   Animation der weiblichen
       Bevölkerung

2467 MASCULINE MILITANCY
    f   Animation masculine
    d   Animation der männ-
       lichen Bevölkerung

2468 MINERS
    f   Mineurs
    d   Grubenarbeiter

2469 NATIONAL
    f   Ressortissant
    d   Staatsbürger

2470 NEW TOWN
    f   Ville nouvelle
    d   Autonomer Stadtteil

2471 OCCUPATIONAL GROUPS
    f   Groups d'emploi
    d   Beschäftigungsgruppen

128

2493 POPULATION
PROJECTION
f  Projection démographique
d  Demographische Projektion;
   Bevölkerungsprojektion

2494 POPULATION TREND
f  Tendance démographique
d  Demographische Entwicklungstendenz

2495 POPULATION OF WORKING AGE
f  Population en âge de travailler
d  Arbeitsfähige Bevölkerung

2496 CLOSED POPULATION
f  Population fermée
d  Geschlossene Bevölkerung

2497 DE FACTO POPULATION;
PRESENT POPULATION
f  Population de fait;
   Population présente
d  De facto Bevölkerung

2498 DE JURE POPULATION
f  Population de jure;
   Population de droit;
   Population légale
d  De jure Bevölkerung

2499 DENSITY OF POPULATION
f  Densité démographique
d  Bevölkerungsdichte

2500 DYNAMICS OF A POPULATION
f  Variation de l'effectif de la population
d  Bevölkerungsänderung

2501 ECONOMICALLY ACTIVE POPULATION;
GAINFULLY OCCUPIED POPULATION
f  Population active
d  Aktive Bevölkerung

2502 FOREST POPULATION
f  Population forestière
d  Waldbevölkerung

2503 OPTIMUM ECONOMIC POPULATION
f  Population économique optimum
d  Wirtschaflich optimale Bevölkerung

2504 OPTIMUM POPULATION LEVEL
f  Niveau optimum de la population
d  Optimales Bevölkerungsniveau

2505 OPTIMUM RATE OF POPULATION GROWTH
f  Taux optimum d'accroissement de la population
d  Optimale Rate des Bevölkerungswachstums

2506 OVERPOPULATION
f  Surpeuplement
d  Überbevölkerung

2507 PROSPECTIVE POPULATION TRENDS
f  Tendances démographiques
d  Demographische Trends

2508 PROSPECTS FOR POPULATION
f  Perspectives démographiques
d  Demographische Perspektiven

2509 RURAL POPULATION
f  Population rurale
d  Ländliche Bevölkerung

2510 SIZE OF POPULATION
f  Volume de la population
d  Bevölkerungsgrösse

2511 STABLE POPULATION
f Population stable
d Stabile Bevölkerung

2512 UNDERPOPULATION
f Sous-peuplement
d Unterbevölkerung

2513 URBAN POPULATION
f Population urbaine
d Städtische Bevölkerung

2514 WAGE EARNING POPU-
LATION
f Population salariée
d Lohnempfangender
Bevölkerungsteil

2515 WORKING AGE POPULA-
TION;
POPULATION OF WORKING
AGE
f Population en âge de
travailler;
Population en âge
d'activité
d Bevölkerung im Arbeits-
alter

2516 POSITION CLASSIFICATION
f Classification des emplois
d Klassifizierung der
Beschäftigten

2617 PRODUCTIVE MAN-HOURS
f Heures de travail
productif
d Produktive Arbeitsstunden

2518 PROFESSIONAL GROUPS
f Catégories des spécia-
listes;
Groupes professionnels
d Berufsgruppen

2519 PUBLIC HEALTH
f Santé publique
d Öffentliches Gesundheits-
wesen

2520 PUBLIC HEALTH
ENGINEERING
f Technologie sanitaire
d Sanitäre Technologie

2521 REFUGEES
f Réfugiés
d Flüchtlinge

2522 PROBLEMS OF REFUGEES
f Problèmes des réfugiés
d Flüchtlingsprobleme

2523 NATIONAL REGISTER
f Registre national
d Nationales Register

2524 RESETTLEMENT
f Réinstallation
d Umsiedlung

2525 RETRAINING
f Réadaptation
professionnelle
d Umschulung

2526 SANITARY CONDITIONS
f Conditions sanitaires
d Sanitäre Bedingungen

2527 SCARCITY IN SKILLS
f Pénurie de compétences
d Mangel an Kader

2528 SHORTAGE OF STAFF
f Manque de personnel
d Personalmangel

2529 COST OF SICKNESS
f Coût de la maladie
d Krankheitskosten

2530 SLUM CLEARANCE;
IMPROVEMENT OF TOWNS
f Elimination des taudis;
Aménagement des bidon-
villes
d Slumeliminierung

2531 SOCIAL AID;
SOCIAL ASSISTANCE;
SOCIAL RELIEF
f  Aide sociale
d  Soziale Hilfe

2532 SOCIAL ASPECTS
f  Aspects sociaux
d  Soziale Aspekte

2533 SOCIAL CLASSES
f  Classes sociales;
Stratifications sociales
d  Soziale Klassen

2534 SOCIAL ENVIRONMENT
f  Milieu social
d  Soziale Umgebung

2535 SOCIAL INSURANCE
f  Assurances sociales
d  Soziale Versicherung

2536 SOCIAL JUSTICE
f  Justice sociale
d  Soziale Gerechtigkeit

2537 SOCIAL MOBILITY
f  Mobilité sociale
d  Soziale Mobilität

2538 SOCIAL POLICY
f  Politique sociale
d  Sozialpolitik

2539 SOCIAL POSITION
f  Position sociale
d  Soziale Stellung

2540 SOCIAL PROMOTER;
EXTENSION WORKER
f  Animateur
d  Animateur

2541 SOCIAL SECURITY
f  Sécurité sociale
d  Soziale Sicherheit

2542 SOCIAL SECURITY
CONTRIBUTIONS
f  Côtisations de sécurité
sociale

d  Beiträge für soziale
Sicherheit

2543 SOCIAL SITUATION
f  Situation sociale
d  Soziale Situation

2544 SOCIAL STATUS
f  Statut social
d  Sozialer Status

2545 SOCIAL STRATIFICATION
f  Stratification sociale
d  Soziale Stratifikation

2546 SOCIAL WELFARE
INSTITUTIONS
f  Oeuvres d'assistance
sociale
d  Sozialeinrichtungen

2547 BASIC SOCIAL SECURITY
PROVISION
f  Régime élémentaire de
sécurité sociale
d  Elementares System
für soziale Sicherheit

2548 SOCIOGRAPHY
f  Sociographie
d  Soziographie

2549 SUB-CONTRACTORS
f  Sous-traitants
d  Heimarbeiter

2550 SYSTEMS OF REMUNERA-
TION
f  Système de rémunération
d  Remunerationssystem

2551 TECHNICIANS
f  Techniciens
d  Techniker

2552 TOWN DWELLERS;
URBAN POPULATION
f  Couche urbaine
d  Stadtbewohner

| | | | | |
|---|---|---|---|---|
| 2553 | TRANSMIGRATION<br>f Passage à travers un<br>territoire<br>d Transmigration | | 2564 | VILLAGE LEVEL<br>f Niveau du village<br>d Dorfniveau |

2553 TRANSMIGRATION
    f  Passage à travers un
       territoire
    d  Transmigration

2554 TYPE OF ACTIVITY
    f  Type d'activité
    d  Aktivitätsart

2555 TYPE OF SKILL
    f  Type de compétence
    d  Art der beruflichen
       Kompetenz

2556 UNDER-EMPLOYMENT
    f  Sous-emploi
    d  Unterbeschäftigung

2557 DISGUISED UNEMPLOY-
    MENT
    f  Chômage déguisé;
       Chômage latent
    d  Versteckte Arbeitslosig-
       keit

2558 INVISIBLE UNEMPLOYMENT
    f  Chômage invisible
    d  Unsichtbare Arbeits-
       losigkeit

2559 UNION MEMBERS
    f  Membres de syndicats
    d  Gewerkschaftsmitglieder

2560 INTERNATIONAL TRADE
    UNIONS
    f  Syndicats internationaux
    d  Internationale Gewerk-
       schaften

2561 UNIONIST
    f  Syndicaliste
    d  Gewerkschaftsmitglied

2562 URBANIZATION
    f  Urbanisation
    d  Verstädterung;
       Urbanisierung

2563 EXISTING VACANCIES
    f  Postes vacants
    d  Bestehende Arbeitsplätze

2564 VILLAGE LEVEL
    f  Niveau du village
    d  Dorfniveau

2565 NEARBY VILLAGES
    f  Villages environnants
    d  Nachbardörfer

2566 VOTING RIGHT
    f  Droit de vote
    d  Wahlrecht

2567 WAGE CONTROL
    f  Contrôle des salaires
    d  Lohnkontrolle

2568 WAGE COST
    f  Coût salarial
    d  Lohnkosten

2569 WAGE DEMANDS;
    WAGE REQUIREMENTS
    f  Revendications
       salariales
    d  Lohnforderungen

2570 WAGE DRIFT
    f  Dérapage des salaires
    d  Lohnunterschied

2571 WAGE EARNERS
    f  Salariés
    d  Lohnempfänger

2572 WAGE FREEZE
    f  Blocage des salaires
    d  Lohnstop

2573 WAGE INCREASE
    f  Augmentation des
       salaires
    d  Lohnerhöhungen

2574 WAGE INDEX
    f  Indice des salaires
    d  Lohnindex

2575 WAGE LEVEL
    f  Niveau des salaires
    d  Lohnniveau

2576 WAGE PLANNING
    f  Planification des salaires
    d  Lohnplanung

2577 WAGE POLICY;
       PAYROLL POLICY
    f  Politique des salaires
    d  Lohnpolitik

2578 WAGE-PRICE SPIRAL
    f  Course des salaires et
       des prix
    d  Lohn-Preis Spirale

2579 WAGE STRUCTURE
    f  Structure de salaires;
       Barème de salaires
    d  Lohnstruktur

2580 WAGES AND SALARIES
    f  Salaires et traitements
    d  Löhne und Gehälter

2581 MINIMUM LEGAL WAGE
    f  Salaire minimal légal
    d  Gesetzlicher Mindestlohn

2582 REAL WAGE
    f  Salaire réel
    d  Reallohn

2583 SUBSISTENCE WAGE
    f  Salaire de subsistance
    d  Subsistenzlohn

2584 HARMONIZATION OF
       WAGES
    f  Harmonisation des
       salaires
    d  Lohnangleichung

2585 WELFARE OF THE AGED
    f  Aide aux vieillards
    d  Altersfürsorge

2586 CHILD WELFARE
    f  Bien-être de l'enfance
    d  Wohlfahrt der Kinder

2587 CHILDREN'S WELFARE
    f  Protection de l'enfance
    d  Schutz der Kinder

2588 SOCIAL WELFARE
    f  Protection sociale;
       Bien-être sociale
    d  Sozialer Schutz;
       Soziale Wohlfahrt

2589 SOCIAL WELFARE
       INSTITUTIONS
    f  Etablissements d'utilité
       sociale
    d  Soziale Wohlfahrts-
       organisationen

2590 SOCIAL WELFARE
       SERVICES
    f  Services d'assistance
       sociale;
       Prestations sociales
    d  Soziale Wohlfahrts-
       einrichtungen

2591 WOMEN'S LABOUR
    f  Travail des femmes
    d  Frauenarbeit

2592 WOMEN'S ASSOCIATIONS
    f  Associations féminines
    d  Frauenbünde

2593 WORK CONTRACT
    f  Contrat de travail
    d  Arbeitsvertrag

2594 WORK PROGRAMME
    f  Programme de travail
    d  Arbeitsprogramm

2595 WORK SAFETY
    f  Protection du travail
    d  Arbeitsschutz

2596 WORKER MOVEMENT
    f  Mouvement ouvrier
    d  Arbeiterbewegung

2597 DAILY PAID WORKERS;
       DAY WORKERS
    f  Travailleurs payés à
       la journée
    d  Taglöhner

2598 FARM WORKERS
    f  Ouvriers agricoles
    d  Landarbeiter

2599 ILLITERATE WORKERS
    f  Ouvriers illettrés
    d  Lese- und schreibunkun-
       dige Arbeiter

2600 MIGRANT WORKERS
    f  Travailleurs migrateurs
    d  Wanderarbeiter

2601 MULTI-PURPOSE WORKER
    f  Assistant polyvalent
    d  Polyvalenter Assistent

2602 SEASONAL WORKERS
    f  Travailleurs saisonniers
    d  Saisonarbeiter

2603 WORKING CAPACITY
    f  Capacité de travail
    d  Arbeitskapazität

2604 WORKING LIFE
    f  Vie active
    d  Aktive Lebensspanne

2605 WORKING PARTY
    f  Groupe de travail
    d  Arbeitsgruppe

2606 WORKING TOOLS
    f  Instruments de travail
    d  Arbeitsinstrumente

2607 YOUTH EDUCATION
    f  Formation des jeunes
    d  Jugendbildung

2608 YOUTH MOVEMENT
    f  Mouvement de la jeunesse
    d  Jugendbewegung

2609 YOUTH SERVICE
    f  Organisation de jeunesse
    d  Jugendorganisation

2610 NATIONAL YOUTH
    SERVICE
    f  Service national de la
       jeunesse
    d  Nationaler Jugenddienst

# XI
## ECONOMIC ETHNOLOGY
## ETHNOLOGIE ECONOMIQUE
## WIRTSCHAFTSETHNOLOGIE

2611 ACCULTURATION;
CULTURE CONTACTS;
CULTURE CLASH
f  Acculturation;
THURNWALD
d  Akkulturation;
Kultureller Ausgleich;
KRICKEBERG

2612 ACHIEVEMENT MOTIVATION
f  Motivation
d  Beweggrund;
Motivation

2613 NON-ECONOMIC
ACTIVITY
f  Activité non-économique
d  Nicht-wirtschaftliche
Aktivität

2614 ADJUSTMENT PROCESS
f  Processus d'ajustement
d  Anpassungsprozess

2615 AFRICANIZATION
f  Africanisation
d  Afrikanisierung

2616 AFRICAN PARTICULARISM
f  Particularisme africain
d  Afrikanischer
Partikularismus

2617 AFRICAN POPULATION
f  Population africaine
d  Afrikanische Bevölkerung

2618 AFRICAN SOCIETY
f  Société africaine
d  Afrikanische Gesellschaft

2619 SOCIO-POLITICAL
ANALYSIS
f  Analyse socio-politique
d  Soziopolitische
Analyse

2620 ANIMISM
f  Animisme
d  Animismus

2621 CULTURAL ANTHROPOLOGY
f  Anthropologie culturelle
d  Völkerkunde ohne
soziologische Aspekte;
Kulturanthropologie

2622 SOCIAL ANTHROPOLOGY
f  Anthropologie sociale
d  Soziologische Völkerkunde

2623 BASKET MAKING
f  Vannerie
d  Korbflechterei

2624 ECONOMIC BEHAVIOUR
f  Comportement économique
d  Wirtschaftliches
Verhalten

2625 MODIFICATION OF
BEHAVIOUR
f  Modification du comportement
d  Veränderung der Ver-
haltensweiss

2626 CASTE
f  Caste
d  Kaste

2627 CONSUMPTION CELL
f  Cellule de consommation
d  Konsumzelle

2628 PRODUCTION CELL
    f  Cellule de production
    d  Produktionszelle

2629 CHIEFTAINSHIPS
    f  Chefferies
    d  Chefferien

2630 CITIZENSHIP
    f  Citoyenneté
    d  Staatsbürgerschaft

2631 SPECIAL CLOTHING
INDUSTRIES
    f  Industrie locale d'habille-
       ment
    d  Lokale Bekleidungs-
       industrie

2632 COLOUR BAR
    f  Discrimination raciale
    d  Rassische Diskriminierung

2633 TRADITIONAL COMMODITY
    f  Marchandise traditionnelle
    d  Traditionelle Waren

2634 COMMUNITY SPIRIT
    f  Esprit communautaire
    d  Gemeinschaftsgeist

2635 REFORM OF THE
COMMUNITY
    f  Réforme communautaire
    d  Kommunalreform

2636 COMPLEMENTARY
EFFECTS
    f  Effets complémentaires
    d  Komplementäreffekte

2637 INFERIORITY COMPLEX
    f  Complexe d'infériorité
    d  Minderwertigkeitskomplex

2638 SUPERIORITY COMPLEX
    f  Complexe de supériorité
    d  Superioritätskomplex

2639 CLIMATIC CONDITIONS
    f  Conditions climatologiques
    d  Klimatische Bedingungen

2640 LOCAL CONDITIONS
    f  Conditions locales
    d  Lokale Bedingungen

2641 CONSUMER GROUPS
    f  Groupes de consomma-
       teurs
    d  Konsumentengruppen

2642 HOME CONSUMPTION
    f  Consommation domestique
    d  Inlandkonsum

2643 SELF-CONSUMPTION
    f  Auto-consommation
    d  Eigenkonsum

2644 AFRICAN CONTEXT
    f  Contexte africain
    d  Afrikanisches Milieu

2645 GOLDSMITH'S CRAFT
    f  Orfèvrerie
    d  Goldschmiedehandwerk

2646 RURAL CRAFT
    f  Artisanat rural
    d  Ländliches Handwerk

2647 CULTURE
    f  Civilisation
    d  Sozio-kulturelle Struktur

2648 CULTURE AREA
    f  Région d'une culture
    d  Kulturareal

2649 CULTURE CONTACTS
    f  Contacts de culture
    d  Kulturelle Kontakte

2650 AFRICAN CULTURES
    f  Civilisations africaines
    d  Afrikanische Kulturen

2651 NATIVE CULTURE
    f  Civilisation indigène
    d  Eingeborenenkultur

| | | | |
|---|---|---|---|
| 2652 | PREINDUSTRIAL CULTURE<br>f Civilisation pré-industrielle<br>d Prä-industrielle Kultur | 2665 | CULTURAL RELATIONS<br>f Relations culturelles<br>d Kulturbeziehungen |
| 2653 | PRELITERATE CULTURES<br>f Cultures prélitrées<br>d Schriftlose Kulturen | 2666 | CULTURAL STIMULATION<br>f Stimulants culturels<br>d Kulturelle Stimuli |
| 2654 | SHIFTING CULTURE<br>f Transformation culturelle<br>d Kultur im Wandel | 2667 | CULTURAL SUMMARY<br>f Sommaire culturel<br>d Kulturelle Gesamtschau |
| 2655 | SUB-CULTURE<br>f Sous-culture<br>d Subkultur | 2668 | CULTURAL VALUES<br>f Valeurs culturelles<br>d Kulturelle Werte |
| 2656 | TRIBAL CULTURE<br>f Civilisation tribale<br>d Stammeskultur | 2669 | CUSTOMS<br>f Coutumes<br>d Sitten |
| 2657 | CULTURAL ASSISTANCE<br>f Assistance culturelle<br>d Kulturelle Hilfe | 2670 | PATTERN OF CULTURE<br>f Formes de culture<br>d Kulturgefüge |
| 2658 | CULTURAL BARRIER<br>f Obstacle culturel<br>d Kulturelle Hindernisse | 2671 | TRADITIONAL CULTURE<br>METHODS<br>f Méthodes de cultures<br>traditionnelles |
| 2659 | CULTURAL CHANGE<br>f Changement culturel<br>d Kultureller Wandel | | d Traditionelle Bebauungs-<br>methoden |
| 2660 | CULTURAL GOALS<br>f Buts culturels<br>d Kulturelle Ziele | 2672 | DECULTURATION<br>f Déculturation<br>d Dekulturation |
| 2661 | CULTURAL LAG<br>f Décalage culturel<br>d Kulturelle Diskrepanz | 2673 | DIETARY DEFICIENCY<br>f Déficiences du régime<br>alimentaire<br>d Mangelhafte Ernährung |
| 2662 | CULTURAL PARTICIPATION<br>f Participation culturelle<br>d Kulturelle Teilnahme | 2674 | PROTEIN DEFICIENCY<br>f Malnutrition protéique<br>d Protein-Unterernährung |
| 2663 | CULTURAL PATTERN;<br>PATTERN OF CULTURE<br>f Structure d'une civilisation<br>d Stil einer Kultur | 2675 | COMPLEMENTARY DEVE-<br>LOPMENT<br>f Développement complé-<br>mentaire<br>d Komplementäre Ent- |
| 2664 | CULTURAL POTENTIAL<br>f Possibilités culturelles<br>d Kulturelle Möglichkeiten | | wicklung |

2676 SOCIOLOGY OF DEVELOP-
MENT
f  Sociologie du développement
d  Entwicklungssoziologie

2677 DIFFICULTIES OF
ADAPTATION
f  Difficultés d'adaptation
d  Anpassungsschwierig-
keiten

2678 DOMESTIC WORK
f  Travaux ménagers
d  Hausarbeit

2679 STANDARDIZED DWELLING
f  Habitation-type;
Habitation témoin
d  Wohnungstype

2680 ECONOMIC CENTRES
f  Centres économiques
d  Wirtschaftszentren

2681 ECONOMIC REQUIREMENTS
f  Exigences économiques
d  Ökonomische Erforder-
nisse

2682 ECONOMIC SOCIOLOGY
f  Sociologie économique:
d  Wirtschaftssoziologie

2683 ECONOMIC WAR
f  Bataille économique;
BOURGUIBA
d  Wirtschaftskampf

2684 LOCAL ELITE
f  Elite locale
d  Lokale Elite

2685 REVOLUTIONARY ELITE
f  Elite révolutionnaire
d  Revolutionäre Elite

2686 HUMAN ENVIRONMENT
f  Milieu humain
d  Menschliche Umgebung

2687 NATURAL ENVIRONMENT
f  Milieu naturel
d  Natürliche Umgebung

2688 NON-TRADITIONAL
ENVIRONMENT
f  Milieu extra-coutumier
d  Untraditionelle Umgebung

2689 PHYSICAL ENVIRONMENT
f  Milieu physique
d  Physische Umgebung

2690 SOCIAL ENVIRONMENT
f  Milieu social
d  Soziales Milieu

2691 TRADITIONAL ENVIRON-
MENT
f  Milieu coutumier;
Milieu traditionnel
d  Traditionelle Umgebung

2692 THERAPY OF THE
"NORMAL ENVIRONMENT"
f  Thérapie du "milieu
habituel"
d  "Milieugerechte" Thera-
pie

2693 ETHNIC GROUPS
f  Groupes ethniques
d  Ethnische Gruppen

2694 ETHNIC PROBLEMS
f  Problèmes ethniques
d  Ethnische Probleme

2695 APPLIED ETHNOLOGY;
PRACTICAL ETHNOLOGY
f  Ethnologie appliquée
d  Angewandte Völkerkunde;
Ethnosoziologie;
MANNDORF

2696 PROSPECTIVE ETHNOLOGY
f  Ethnologie prospective
d  Prospektive Völkerkunde;
Prospektive Ethnologie

2697 ETHNOGRAPHIC
SITUATION
   f  Situation ethnographique
   d  Ethnographische
      Situation

2698 EUROPEANIZATION
   f  Européanisation
   d  Europäisierung

2699 TRADITIONAL EXCHANGE
   f  Echange traditionnel
   d  Traditioneller Handel

2700 GEOGRAPHICAL FACTORS
   f  Facteurs géographiques
   d  Geographische Faktoren

2701 PSYCHOLOGICAL FACTORS
   f  Facteurs psychologiques
   d  Psychologische Faktoren

2702 SOCIO-ECONOMIC FACTORS
   f  Facteurs socio-écono-
      miques
   d  Sozio-ökonomische Fakto-
      ren

2703 FAMILY ECONOMY
   f  Economie de famille
   d  Familienwirtschaft

2704 FAMILY ORGANIZATION
   f  Organisation familiale
   d  Familienorganisation

2705 FAMILY UNITY
   f  Unité de famille
   d  Familieneinheit

2706 EXTENDED FAMILY
   f  Famille étendue
   d  Grossfamilie

2707 WESTERN TYPE OF
FAMILY
   f  Famille de style occiden-
      tal
   d  Familie westlichen
      Stils

2708 FAMILIAL GROUP
   f  Groupe familial
   d  Familiengruppe

2709 FAMINE
   f  Famine
   d  Hungersnot

2710 FETISHISM
   f  Fétichisme
   d  Fetischismus

2711 FEUDAL STRUCTURES
   f  Structures féodales
   d  Feudalstrukturen

2712 PHYSICAL AND MENTAL
FITNESS
   f  Santé physique et
      mentale
   d  Physische und mentale
      Gesundheit

2713 FOOD HABITS
   f  Coutumes d'alimenta-
      tions
   d  Ernährungsgewohnheiten

2714 FOOD NEEDS
   f  Besoins alimentaires
   d  Nahrungsbedarf

2715 FOOD PREPARATION
   f  Préparation de la
      nourriture
   d  Nahrungszubereitung

2716 FOREST PRODUCTS
   f  Produits forestiers
   d  Waldprodukte;
      Forstprodukte

2717 NATIONAL FRAMEWORK
   f  Cadre national
   d  Nationaler Rahmen

2718 HABITS
   f  Usages
   d  Gewohnheiten

2719 ANCIENT HABITS
    f  Usages ancestraux
    d  Alte Gebräuche

2720 ILL HEALTH
    f  Santé déficiente
    d  Mangelnde Gesundheit

2721 HOME ECONOMICS
    f  Economie domestique
    d  Heimwirtschaft

2722 CIRCULAR HOUSE
    f  Maison annulaire
    d  Rundhaus

2723 HOUSING
    f  Logement;
       Habitat
    d  Wohnsystem

2724 LOW-COST HOUSING
    f  Habitations à bon marché;
       Habitations à loyer
       modéré
       (HLM)
    d  Preiswertes Wohnsystem

2725 SELF-HELP HOUSING
    f  Petite construction
       individuelle;
       Auto-construction
    d  Eigenkonstruktion

2726 HUMAN ELEMENTS
    f  Eléments humains
    d  Menschliche Faktoren

2727 HUMAN RELATIONS
    f  Relations humaines
    d  Menschliche Beziehungen

2728 HUMAN REQUIREMENTS
    f  Exigences humaines
    d  Menschliche Erforder-
       nisse

2729 HUNGER PROBLEMS
    f  Problèmes de la faim
    d  Hungerprobleme

2730 GRATIFICATION AND
    CONTROL OF HUNGER
    f  Satisfaction et contrôle
       de la faim
    d  Befriedung und Kontrolle
       von Hungerproblemen

2731 GEOGRAPHICAL LOCATION
    f  Emplacement géographique
    d  Geographische Lokali-
       sierung

2732 GROUP COHESION
    f  Cohésion de groupes
    d  Soziale Kohärenz

2733 ABORIGINAL GROUPS
    f  Groupes aborigènes
    d  Aborigene Gruppen

2734 JEWELRY MANUFACTURE
    f  Fabrication de bijoux
    d  Schmuckherstellung

2735 IMPOVERISHMENT
    f  Appauvrissement
    d  Verarmung

2736 ECONOMIC INDEPENDANCE
    f  Indépendance économique
    d  Wirtschaftliche Unab-
       hängigkeit

2737 SOCIO-ECONOMIC INFRA-
    STRUCTURE
    f  Infrastructure socio-
       économique
    d  Sozio-ökonomische
       Infrastruktur

2738 INHABITANTS
    f  Habitants
    d  Einwohner

2739 CLAN INSTITUTION
    f  Institution tribale
    d  Stammesinstitution

2740 FEUDAL INSTITUTION
    f  Institution féodale
    d  Feudalinstitution

2741 INSTITUTIONS FOR
 MODERNIZATION
  f Institutions de
   modernisation
  d Institutionen zur
   Modernisierung

2742 ISLAM
  f Islâm;
   Islame
  d Islam

2743 BLACK ISLAM
  f Islâm noire;
   MONTEIL
  d Schwarzer Islam

2744 "IZATION" PROBLEMS;
 TINBERGEN
  f Problèmes "d'isation"
  d "Isierungs"-Probleme

2745 KINSHIP
  f Liens de parenté
  d Verwandschaft

2746 KINSHIP RELATIONSHIP
  f Rapports lignagers
  d Verwandtschaftsbezie-
   hungen

2747 LAND CHIEF
  f Chef de terre;
   Maître du champ
  d "Land-Häuptling"

2748 COMMON LAW;
 CUSTOMARY LAW
  f Droit coutumier
  d Gewohnheitsrecht

2749 ISLAMIC LAW
  f Droit islamique
  d Islamisches Recht

2750 NATIONAL LANGUAGE
  f Langue nationale
  d Nationalsprache

2751 PRINCIPAL LANGUAGES
  f Principales langues

  d Hauptverkehrssprachen

2752 TEACHING LANGUAGE
  f Langue d'enseignement
  d Unterrichtssprache

2753 VERNACULAR LANGUAGES;
 INDIGENOUS LANGUAGES
  f Langues vernaculaires
  d Eingeborenensprachen

2754 COLONIAL LEGISLATION
  f Législation coloniale
  d Koloniale Gesetzgebung

2755 MODERN LEGISLATION
  f Législation moderne
  d Moderne Gesetzgebung

2756 MULTIPLICITY OF LEGAL
 SYSTEMS
  f Multiplicité juridique
  d Vielfalt der Rechts-
   systeme

2757 LIFE EXPECTANCY
  f Espérances de vie
  d Lebenserwartung

2758 LINGUISTIC AREAS
  f Régions linguistiques
  d Sprachgebiete

2759 RURAL LIVING
  f Vie rurale
  d Ländlicher Lebensstil

2760 URBAN LIVING
  f Vie urbaine
  d Städtischer Lebensstil

2761 PATTERNS OF LIVING
  f Modes de vie
  d Lebensstile

2762 LOCAL CONSTRAINTS
  f Obstacles de caractère
   local
  d Lokale Hindernisse

2763 LOCAL STUDIES
    f  Etudes locales
    d  Lokalstudien

2764 LOST-WAX METHOD
    f  Méthode de la cire
       perdue
    d  Technik der verlorenen
       Form

2765 MAGIC TOOL
    f  Instrument magique
    d  Magisches Werkzeug

2766 TROPICAL MEDICINE
    f  Médicine tropicale
    d  Tropische Medizin

2767 MEDINA;
    NATIVE QUARTER
    f  Médina
    d  Medina;
       Eingeborenenviertel

2768 METAL WORK
    f  Taillanderie
    d  Schmiedehandwerk

2769 NATIONAL MINORITIES
    f  Minorités nationales
    d  Nationale Minderheiten

2770 MOTHER TONGUE
    f  Langue maternelle
    d  Muttersprache

2771 ETHNIC NATIONALISM
    f  Nationalisme ethnique
    d  Ethnischer Nationalismus

2772 PAN-ETHNIC NATIONALISM
    f  Nationalisme pan-ethnique
    d  Pan-ethnischer
       Nationalismus

2773 TRADITIONAL NATIVE
    AUTHORITIES
    f  Autorités indigènes
       traditionnelles
    d  Traditionelle Einge-
       borenenautoritäten

2774 NEGRO ARTS
    f  Arts nègres
    d  Negerkunst

2775 NEIGHBOURHOOD
    f  Voisinage
    d  Nachbarschaft

2776 NEIGHBOURHOOD UNIT
    f  Unité de voisinage
    d  Nachbarschaftseinheit

2777 NOMADISM
    f  Nomadisme
    d  Nomadentum

2778 AGRICULTURAL SEMI-
    NOMADISM
    f  Semi-nomadisme agricole
    d  Landwirtschaftliches
       Halbnomadentum

2779 UNDER-NOURISHMENT
    f  Sous-alimentation
    d  Unterernährung

2780 NUTRITION
    f  Régime alimentaire
    d  Ernährung

2781 OBSERVATIONAL ROLE
    f  Rôle d'observation
    d  Beobachtungsrolle

2782 ORGANIZATION OF
    AFRICAN UNITY (O.A.U.)
    f  Organisation de l'Unité
       Africaine (O.U.A.)
    d  Organisation der afri-
       kanischen Einheit

2783 PARASITIC INFECTIONS
    f  Maladies parasitaires
    d  Parasitäre Krankheiten

2784 PATERNALISM
    f  Paternalisme
    d  Paternalismus

2785 DE-RURALIZED PEASANT
 f Paysan dépaysanné
 d Dem Bauerntum entfrem-
   dete bäuerliche Elemente

2786 PRE-EUROPEAN PERIOD
 f Période prae-européenne
 d Vor-europäische Periode

2787 PILOT VILLAGE
 f Village pilote
 d Musterdorf

2788 POLYGAMY
 f Polygamie
 d Polygamie

2789 POTTERY
 f Poterie
 d Töpferei

2790 PRESERVATION AND STO-
   RAGE OF FOOD
 f Conservation et emmaga-
   sinage des aliments
 d Konservierung und Lagerhaltung von Nahrungs-
   mitteln

2791 MOTIVATED PRESTIGE
 f Prestige motivé
 d Soziale Geltung

2792 PROCESSING OF BASIC
   MATERIALS
 f Transformation de
   matières primaires
 d Verarbeitung von
   Rohmaterialien

2793 PROFESSIONAL ETHIC
 f Ethique professionnelle
 d Berufsethik

2794 RACES
 f Races
 d Rassen;
   Volksgruppen

2795 RACE RELATIONS;
   RACIAL RELATIONS
 f Relations raciales
 d Rassische Beziehungen

2796 RACIAL AFFINITIES
 f Affinités raciales
 d Rassische Ähnlichkeiten

2797 RACIAL DIFFERENCES
 f Différences raciales
 d Rassische Verschieden-
   heiten

2798 RACIAL FACTORS
 f Facteurs raciaux
 d Rassische Faktoren

2799 MULTI-RACIAL COUNTRY
 f Pays à races multiples
 d Viel-rassisches Land

2800 RELIGIOUS LEADERS
 f Chefs religieux
 d Religiöse Führer

2801 RELIGIOUS STRUCTURE
 f Structures religieuses
 d Religionsstruktur

2802 RELIGIOUS TABOO
 f Tabous religieux
 d Religiöse Tabus

2803 PAGAN RELIGION
 f Religion païenne
 d Heidnische Religion

2804 RESIDENTIAL AREA
 f Quartier résidentiel
 d Wohngebiet

2805 SOCIAL RISK
 f Risque social
 d Soziales Risiko

2806 SEA HUNTING
 f Chasse marine
 d Fischjagd

2807 SYSTEM OF SOCIAL
SECURITY
f Régime de sécurité
sociale
d System sozialer
Sicherheit

2808 TRADITIONAL FORM OF
SECURITY
f Sécurité traditionnelle
d Traditionelle Form der
Sicherheit

2809 SELF-SUPPLY
f Auto-fourniture
d Selbstversorgung

2810 SEMI-ARID COUNTRY
f Pays semi-aride
d Semi-arides Land

2811 SETTLEMENT
f Peuplement
d Besiedlung

2812 SETTLEMENT PATTERN
f Structure d'habitat
d Besiedlungsform;
Siedlungsstruktur

2813 SETTLEMENT OF NOMADS
f Fixation des nomades
d Sesshaftmachung der
Nomaden

2814 RELICS OF SLAVERY
f Survivances de
l'esclavage
d Restbestände der
Sklaverei

2815 SLUMS
f Bidonvilles
d Blech- und Bretterhütten

2816 SOCIAL CHANGE
f Changement social;
Evolution sociale
d Sozialer Wandel

2817 CULTURAL CHANGE
f Changement culturel
d Kulturwandel

2818 SOCIAL CONTROL
f Contrôle social
d Soziale Kontrolle

2819 SOCIAL CRISIS
f Crise sociale
d Soziale Krise

2820 SOCIAL DESINTEGRATION
f Désintégration sociale
d Soziale Desintegration

2821 SOCIAL DISORGANIZATION
f Désorganisation sociale
d Soziale Disorganisation

2822 SOCIAL INEQUALITY
f Inégalité sociale
d Soziale Ungleichheit

2823 SOCIAL INTEGRATION
f Intégration sociale
d Soziale Integration

2824 SOCIAL MECHANISM
f Mécanisme social
d Sozialer Mechanismus

2825 SOCIAL OBLIGATIONS
f Obligations sociales
d Soziale Verpflichtungen

2826 SOCIAL PERSONALITY
f Personnalité sociale
d Soziale Persönlichkeit

2827 SOCIAL RESPONSIBILITY
f Responsabilité sociale
d Soziale Verantwortung

2828 SOCIAL SNOBBERY
f Snobisme social
d Sozialer Snobismus

2829 SOCIAL STRATIFICATION
f Stratification sociale
d Soziale Struktur

2830   SOCIAL TRANSITION
 f Transition sociale
 d Soziale Übergangsphase

2831   SOCIAL VALUES
 f Valeurs sociales
 d Sozialwerte

2832   TRADITIONAL SOCIETY
 f Société traditionnelle
 d Traditionelle Gesellschaft

2833   ISLAMIC SOCIOLOGY
 f Sociologie islamique
 d Islamische Soziologie

2834   RURAL SOCIOLOGY
 f Sociologie rurale
 d Ruralsoziologie

2835   URBAN SOCIOLOGY
 f Sociologie urbaine
 d Urbane Soziologie

2836   CHANGE IN STATUS
 f Modification des status
 d Statusänderung

2837   STONE INDUSTRY
 f Industrie de la pierre
 d Steinbearbeitung

2838   EMOTIONAL STRESS
 f Contrainte émotionnelle
 d Psychische Spannung

2839   COLONIAL STRUCTURE
 f Structure coloniale
 d Koloniale Struktur

2840   SOCIO-ECONOMIC
  STRUCTURE
 f Structure socio-écono-
  mique
 d Sozio-ökonomische
  Struktur

2841   STRUCTURAL IMBALANCE
 f Déséquilibre structural
 d Strukturelles Ungleich-
  gewicht

2842   STRUCTURAL MUTATION
 f Mutation structurale
 d Strukturelle Mutation

2843   STRUCTURAL PROBLEM
 f Problème structural
 d Strukturelles Problem

2844   STRUCTURAL REORGANI-
  ZATION
 f Réorganisation
  structurale
 d Strukturelle Reorganisa-
  tion

2845   SUBORDINATION OF
  ECONOMICS
 f Subordination de
  l'économie
 d Unterordnung der
  Wirtschaft

2846   LOCAL SUBSISTENCE
 f Subsistence locale
 d Lokale Subsistenz

2847   SURROUNDINGS
 f Milieu
 d Umgebung

2848   MATRILINEAL SYSTEM
 f Système matrilinéaire
 d Matrilineares System

2849   PATRILINEAL SYSTEM
 f Système patrilinéaire
 d Patrilineares System

2850   SOCIO-ECONOMIC SYSTEM
 f Système socio-économique
 d Sozio-ökonomisches
  System

2851   TANNERY
 f Tannerie
 d Gerberei

2852   TRADITIONAL ECONOMY
 f Economie traditionnelle
 d Traditionelle Wirtschaft

2853 SOCIO-CULTURAL
TRENDS
f   Tendances socio-cultu-
relles
d   Sozio-kulturelle Tendenzen

2854 TRIBE
f   Tribu
d   Stamm

2855 TRIBALISM;
ETHNICAL NATIONALISM
f   Tribalisme;
Nationalisme ethnique
d   Stammesnationalismus;
Tribalismus

2856 TRIBAL CUSTOMS
f   Coutumes tribales
d   Stammesgewohnheiten

2857 TRIBAL SEPARATISM
f   Séparatisme tribal
d   Stammesseparatismus

2858 TRIBAL SOCIETY
f   Société tribale
d   Stammesgesellschaft

2859 TRIBAL TIES
f   Liens tribaux
d   Tribale Bindungen

2860 DETRIBALIZATION
f   Détribalisation
d   Detribalisierung;
Stammesentfremdung

2861 TSETSE-FLY CONTROL
f   Lutte contre la mouche
tsé-tsé
d   Tse-Tse Fliege Kontrolle

2862 ANTI-ECONOMIC VALUE
f   Valeur anti-économique
d   Anti-wirtschaftlicher
Wert

2863 SOCIAL VALUE
f   Valeur sociale
d   Sozialer Wert

2864 WEAVING
f   Tissage
d   Weberei

2865 HANDLOOM WEAVING
f   Tissage à la main
d   Handweberei

2866 POWER-LOOM WEAVING
f   Tissage mécanique
d   Mechanisches Weben

2867 CO-WIVES
f   Co-épouses
d   Nebenfrauen

2868 WOOD WORKING
f   Travail du bois
d   Holzbearbeitung

2869 SCULPTURE IN WOOD
f   Sculpture sur bois
d   Holzschnitzerei

2870 WORK IN BONE, HORN
AND SHELL
f   Travail en os, en corne
et en coquillage
d   Arbeit in Knochen,
Horn und Muscheln

2871 WOMEN'S PLACE IN
SOCIETY
f   Condition de la femme
d   Stellung der Frau

2872 INCREASE IN THE YIELD
f   Relèvement du rendement
d   Ertragserhöhung

2873 ZONING
f   Zonage;
Réglementation de
l'usage des superficies
d   Zoneneinteilung

# XII.

## DEVELOPMENT STATISTICS
## STATISTIQUE DU DEVELOPPEMENT
## ENTWICKLUNGSSTATISTIK

74 ACCOUNTING FRAMEWORK
f Cadre comptable
d Rechnungsrahmen

75 ECONOMIC ACCOUNTS
f Comptes économiques
d Wirtschaftskonten

76 AGGREGATE
f Agrégat
d Aggregat

77 FACTOR ANALYSIS
f Analyse factorielle
d Faktorenanalyse

78 NETWORK ANALYSIS;
CRITICAL PATH ANALYSIS
f Méthode du chemin
critique
d Analyse des kritischen
Pfades

79 PARTIAL ANALYSIS
f Analyse partielle
d Partialanalyse

80 PREPARATORY ANALYSIS
f Analyse préparatoire
d Vorbereitungsanalyse

81 SITUATION ANALYSIS
f Analyse de situation
d Situationsanalyse

82 SYSTEM ANALYSIS
f Analyse du système
d Systemanalyse

83 ASSUMPTION
f Hypothèse
d Annahme

2884 AVERAGE
f Moyenne
d Durchschnitt

2885 WEIGHTED AVERAGE
f Moyenne pondérée
d Gewogenes Mittel

2886 WORLD AVERAGE
f Moyenne mondiale
d Weltdurchschnitt

2887 BACKGROUND DOCUMENTS
f Documents de base
d Basisdokumente

2888 BASE PERIOD;
BASIC YEAR;
REFERENCE PERIOD
f Période de base;
Année de base
d Basiszeit;
Basisjahr

2889 BIAS
f Biais
d Verzerrung

2890 BINOMINAL DISTRIBUTION
f Distribution binômale
d Binominalverteilung

2891 BREAK DOWN
f Ventilation
d Aufgliederung

2892 CASE STUDY
f Etude de cas
d Fallstudie

2893 CATALYST
f Catalyseur
d Katalisator

2894  CATEGORY;
CLASS;
GROUP
f  Catégorie;
Classe;
Groupe
d  Kategorie;
Klasse;
Gruppe

2895  CENSUS
f  Recensement;
Dénombrement
d  Zählung

2896  INDUSTRIAL CENSUS
f  Recensement industriel
d  Industrieerhebung

2897  CHARACTERISTIC
f  Caractéristique
d  Merkmal

2898  CLASSIFICATION
f  Classification;
Ventilation
d  Klassifikation;
Klassifizierung;
Gliederung

2899  TABULAR CLASSIFICATION
f  Classification tabulaire
d  Tabularische Klassifikation

2900  EVALUATION COEFFI-
CIENT
f  Coefficient d'évaluation
d  Beurteilungskriterium

2901  SCATTER COEFFICIENT
f  Coefficient de dispersion
d  Streuungskoeffizient

2902  CODING SCHEME;
CODE
f  Code
d  Zahlenschlüssel

2903  COLLECTION OF ORIGINAL
STATISTICAL MATERIAL

f  Collecte des données
de base
d  Gewinnung des statis-
tischen Urmaterials

2904  COMPONENT
f  Composante
d  Komponente

2905  CONSISTENCY TEST
f  Test de cohérence
d  Kohärenztest

2906  CONTINGENCY
f  Contingence
d  Kontingenz

2907  DIRECT CORRELATION
f  Corrélation positive
d  Positive Korrelation

2908  NEGATIVE CORRELATION
f  Corrélation négative
d  Negative Korrelation

2909  COEFFICIENT OF
MULTIPLE CORRELATION
f  Coefficient de corrélatio
multiple
d  Multipler Korrelations-
koeffizient

2910  COVERAGE
f  Couverture
d  Erfassung

2911  CRITERION
f  Critère
d  Kriterium

2912  CROSS-CHECKING OF
STATISTICAL DATA
f  Recoupement des
données statistiques
d  Überprüfung statistische
Daten

2913  CURVE
f  Courbe
d  Kurve

2914 CYCLE
f Cycle
d Zyklus

2915 DATA COLLECTION
f Collecte des données
d Datensammlung

2916 DATA INTERPRETATION
f Interprétation des données statistiques
d Statistische Interpretation

2917 DATA PROCESSING
f Exploitation des données; Dépouillement
d Datenverarbeitung; Datenaufbereitung

2918 BASIC DATA
f Données de base
d Basisdaten

2919 COMPLEMENTARY ITEMS; COMPLEMENTARY DATA
f Données complémentaires
d Zusätzliche Daten

2920 FIELD DATA
f Données recueillies sur le terrain
d Daten von Feldstudien

2921 HISTORICAL DATA
f Données historiques
d Historische Daten

2922 PAST DATA; PAST FIGURES
f Données rétrospectives
d Retrospektive Daten

2923 RAW DATA
f Données brutes
d Rohmaterial

2924 DATE OF REPORT; KEY DATE
f Date de référence
d Berichtszeit

2925 DENSITY
f Densité
d Dichte

2926 ABSOLUTE DEVIATION
f Ecart absolu
d Absolute Abweichung

2927 MEAN DEVIATION
f Ecart moyen
d Durchschnittliche Abweichung

2928 STANDARD DEVIATION
f Ecart type
d Standardabweichung

2929 DIAGRAM
f Diagramme
d Diagramm

2930 DISPERSION; VARIATION; VARIANCE
f Dispersion; Variation; Variance
d Streuung

2931 DOCUMENTATION CENTRE
f Centre de documentation
d Dokumentationszentrum

2932 STATISTICAL DOCUMENTATION
f Documentation statistique
d Statistische Dokumentation

2933 ECONOMETRICS
f Econométrie
d Ökonometrie

2934 ECONOMETRICIAN
f Econ'mètre
d Ökonometriker

2935 EXPERIMENTAL EQUIPMENT
f Dispositif expérimental
d Versuchsmaterial

2936 ERROR BAND;
MARGIN ERROR
f Marge d'erreur;
Intervalle d'erreur
d Fehlerbereich

2937 ABSOLUTE ERROR
f Erreur absolue
d Absoluter Fehler

2938 RANDOM ERROR
f Erreur aléatoire
d Zufallsfehler

2939 SAMPLING ERROR
f Erreur d'échantillonnage
d Stichprobenfehler

2940 SYSTEMATIC ERROR
f Erreur systématique
d Systematischer Fehler

2941 COMPUTATION OF ERRORS
f Calcul d'erreur
d Fehlerberechnung

2942 REALISTIC ESTIMATE
f Estimation réaliste
d Realistische Schätzung

2943 COMPARATIVE EXPERI-
MENT
f Expérimentation comparative
d Komparatives Experiment

2944 FINDINGS
f Résultats
d Ergebnisse

2945 SEASONAL FLUCTUATIONS
f Variations saisonnières;
Fluctuations saisonnières
d Saisonschwankungen

2946 FORECAST
f Prévision
d Ausblick

2947 FREQUENCY DISTRIBUTION
f Distribution de fréquences
d Häufigkeitsverteilung

2948 FREQUENCY FUNCTION
f Fonction de fréquences
d Häufigkeitsfunktion

2949 FREQUENCY MOMENT
f Moment des fréquences;
Moment factoriel
d Häufigkeitsmoment

2950 MEASURE OF
FREQUENCY
f Mesure de fréquence
d Häufigkeitsmass

2951 GRAPH
f Graphique;
Diagramme;
Représentation graphique
d Schaubild

2952 COST-OF-LIVING INDEX
f Indice du coût de la vie
d Lebenskostenindex

2953 GROUP INDEX
f Indice de groupe
d Gruppenindex

2954 PRICE INDEX
f Indice de prix
d Preisindex

2955 PRODUCTION INDEX
f Indice de production
d Produktionsindex

2956 SECTOR INDEX
f Indice selon la méthode
des secteurs
d Sektorindex

2957 STANDARDIZED INDEX
f Indice normalisé
d Standardisierter Index

2958 UNWEIGHTED INDEX
f Indice non-pondéré
d Ungewogener Index

2959 VALUE INDEX
f Indice de valeur
d Wertindex

2960 WEIGHTED INDEX
    f  Indice pondéré
    d  Gewogener Index

2961 STATISTICAL INDICATORS
    f  Indicateurs statistiques
    d  Statistische Indikatoren

2962 INFORMATION FIELD
    f  Domaine d'information
    d  Informationsgebiet

2963 INFORMATION REQUIRE-
MENTS
    f  Besoins en informations
    d  Informationserfordernisse

2964 RELIABLE INFORMATION
    f  Renseignement de source
      sûre
    d  Verlässliche Information

2965 IMPROVEMENT IN ECONO-
MIC INFORMATION
    f  Amélioration de l'infor-
      mation économique
    d  Verbesserung der ökono-
      mischen Information

2966 INPUT-OUTPUT ANALYSIS
    f  Analyse d'input-output;
      Analyse des rapports
      "entrée-sortie"
    d  Input-Output Analyse;
      Intersektorielle Analyse

2967 INPUT-OUTPUT ECONO-
MICS
    f  Economies intersecto-
      rielles
    d  Input-Output

2968 INTERSECTORAL INPUT-
OUTPUT TABLE
    f  Tableau d'échanges
    d  Input-Output Tabelle;
      Intersektorielle Tabelle

2969 INTERPOLATION
    f  Interpolation
    d  Interpolation

2970 PERSONAL INTERVIEW
    f  Interrogatoire direct;
      Enquête directe
    d  Mündliche Befragung

2971 INTERVIEWER;
ENUMERATOR
    f  Enquêteur;
      Recenseur
    d  Interviewer;
      Zähler

2972 LAW OF LARGE NUMBERS
    f  Loi des grands nombres
    d  Gesetz der grossen Zahl

2973 MASS PHENOMENON
    f  Phénomène de masse
    d  Massenerscheinung

2974 MATHEMATICAL
FORMALIZATION
    f  Formalisation
      mathématique
    d  Mathematische Formu-
      lierung

2975 MATHEMATICAL METHODS
IN ECONOMICS
    f  Méthodes mathématiques
      en économie
    d  Wirtschaftsmathematik

2976 MATHEMATICAL MODEL
    f  Modèle mathématique
    d  Mathematisches Modell

2977 MATRICE
    f  Damier
    d  Matrize

2978 MEAN VALUES
    f  Valeurs moyennes
    d  Mittelwerte

2979 WEIGHTED MEAN
    f  Moyenne pondérée
    d  Gewogenes Mittel

2980 UNWEIGHTED MEAN
    f  Moyenne non-pondérée
    d  Ungewogenes Mittel

2981 MEDIAN
    f  Médiane
    d  Medianwert;
       Mittelwert

2982 FIELD METHOD
    f  Méthode d'enquête
    d  Feldmethode

2983 FITTING METHOD
    f  Méthode d'ajustement
    d  Anpassungsmethode

2984 FUNDAMENTAL METHOD
    f  Méthode de base
    d  Basismethode

2985 SCIENTIFIC METHOD
    f  Méthode scientifique
    d  Wissenschaftliche Methode

2986 METHODOLOGY
    f  Méthodologie
    d  Methodologie

2987 MONOGRAPHY
    f  Monographie
    d  Monographie

2988 NORMAL DISTRIBUTION
    f  Distribution normale
    d  Normalverteilung

2989 ORGANIGRAMME
    f  Organigramme
    d  Organigram

2990 OUTPUT PER UNIT OF
    AREA
    f  Productivité à l'hectare
    d  Flächenproduktivität

2991 PARAMETER
    f  Paramètre
    d  Parameter

2992 PERIOD UNDER REVIEW
    f  Période du rapport;
       Période donnée
    d  Berichtszeitraum

2993 GIVEN PERIOD
    f  Période donnée
    d  Berichtszeitraum

2994 POPULATION DATA;
    POPULATION STATISTICS
    f  Données démographiques;
       Statistiques de population
    d  Bevölkerungsstatistik

2995 POPULATION CENSUS
    f  Recensement de popula-
       tion
    d  Volkszählung

2996 INFINITE HOMOGENEOUS
    POPULATION
    f  Population homogène
       infinie
    d  Homogene, unendliche
       Gesamtheit

2997 PREPARATORY WORK
    f  Travaux préliminaires
    d  Vorbereitungsarbeiten

2998 PREVISION
    f  Prévision
    d  Vorausschätzung

2999 PROBABILITY CALCULUS
    f  Calcul de probabilité
    d  Wahrscheinlichkeits-
       rechnung

3000 PROBABILITY SAMPLE
    f  Echantillon probabiliste
    d  Wahrscheinlichkeits-
       stichprobe

3001 PROGRAMMING
    f  Programmation
    d  Programmausarbeitung

3002 PROGRAMMING
TECHNIQUES
f Techniques de la pro-
grammation
d Programmierungstech-
niken

3003 AGRICULTURAL
PROGRAMMING
f Programmation agraire
d Agrarisches Program-
mieren

3004 INDUSTRIAL PROGRAMMING
f Programmation indus-
trielle
d Industrielles
Programmieren

3005 LINEAR PROGRAMMING
f Programmation linéaire
d Lineares Programmieren

3006 PROTOTYPE
f Prototype
d Prototype

3007 PUNCH CARD METHOD
f Procédé par cartes
perforées
d Lochkartenverfahren

3008 QUESTIONNAIRE,
SCHEDULE
f Questionnaire
d Fragebogen

3009 RANDOM COMPONENT
f Composante aléatoire
d Zufallskomponente

3010 RANDOM DISTRIBUTION
f Distribution aléatoire
d Zufallsverteilung

3011 RANDOM SAMPLE
f Echantillon aléatoire
d Zufallsstichprobe

3012 RANDOM SELECTION
f Choix au hasard
d Zufallsauswahl

3013 RATIO
f Rapport;
Quotient
d Verhältniszahl

3014 REGRESSION
f Régression
d Regression

3015 RESEARCH ACTIVITY
f Activités de recherches
d Forschungstätigkeit

3016 RESEARCH CENTRE
f Centre de recherches
d Forschungszentrum

3017 RESEARCH FINDINGS
f Résultats des recherches
d Forschungsresultate

3018 RESEARCH TECHNIQUES
f Techniques de recherches
d Forschungstechniken

3019 APPLIED RESEARCH
f Recherche appliquée
d Angewandte Forschung

3020 BASIC RESEARCH
f Recherche fondamentale
d Grundlagenforschung

3021 ON THE PROBLEM
ORIENTED RESEARCH
f Recherches orientées
sur le problème
d Am Problem orientierte
Forschung

3022 SCIENTIFIC RESEARCH
f Recherche scientifique
d Wissenschaftliche
Forschung

3023 YIELD RESEARCH
f Recherches sur les
rendements
d Ertragsforschung

3024 SAMPLE SURVEY
  f Enquête par sondage;
    Recensement d'essai;
    Recensement préliminaire
  d Stichprobenerhebung;
    Probeerhebung

3025 SUB-SAMPLE
  f Sous-échantillon
  d Unterstichprobe

3026 SAMPLING
  f Echantillonnage
  d Stichprobenverfahren

3027 SAMPLING DISTRIBUTION
  f Distribution d'échantillon-
    nage
  d Stichprobenverteilung

3028 SAMPLING UNIT;
    SAMPLE UNIT
  f Unité d'échantillonnage
  d Auswahleinheit

3029 SCATTER
  f Dispersion
  d Streuung

3030 SCIENTIFIC INSTITUTIONS
  f Institutions scientifiques
  d Wissenschaftliche
    Institutionen

3031 SCIENTIFIC WORK
  f Travail scientifique
  d Wissenschaftliche Arbeit

3032 SIGNIFICANT DIFFERENCE
  f Différence significative
  d Signifikanz

3033 SIMULATION THEORY
  f Théorie de simulation
  d Simulationstheorie

3034 SOCIOGRAMME
  f Sociogramme
  d Soziogramm

3035 THEORETICAL
    SOPHISTICATION
  f Sophistication théorique
  d Theoretische Sophisti-
    kation

3036 INTERNATIONAL STANDARD
  f Normes internationales
  d Internationaler Standard

3037 STANDARDIZATION
  f Normalisation
  d Standardisierung;
    Normalisierung

3038 STATISTICAL ANALYSIS;
    STATISTICAL DECOMPO-
    SITION
  f Analyse statistique;
    Décomposition statistique
  d Statistische Analyse

3039 STATISTICAL CALCULA-
    TIONS
  f Calculs statistiques
  d Statistische Berechnungen

3040 STATISTICAL EVALUATION
  f Estimation statistique
  d Statistische Beurteilung

3041 STATISTICAL METHODS
  f Méthodes statistiques
  d Statistische Methoden

3042 STATISTICAL OBSERVA-
    TIONS
  f Observations statistiques
  d Statistische Beobachtungen

3043 STATISTICAL ORGANIZA-
    TION
  f Organisation statistique
  d Statistische Organisation

3044 STATISTICAL POPULATION
    UNIVERSE
  f Population universe
  d Statistische Masse

3045 STATISTICAL SURVEY
 f  Enquête statistique
 d  Statistische Erhebung

3046 STATISTICAL SERIES
 f  Séries statistiques
 d  Statistische Reihen

3047 STATISTICAL TABLES
 f  Tableaux statistiques
 d  Statistische Tabellen

3048 STATISTICAL TEST
 f  Test statistique
 d  Statistischer Test

3049 STATISTICAL YEAR BOOK
 f  Annuaire statistique
 d  Statistisches Jahrbuch

3050 AGRICULTURAL STATIS-
 TICS
 f  Statistiques agricoles
 d  Agrarstatistik

3051 ANALYTICAL STATISTICS
 f  Statistiques analytiques
 d  Analytische Statistik

3052 APPLIED STATISTICS
 f  Statistiques appliquées
 d  Angewandte Statistik

3053 BIRTH STATISTICS
 f  Statistique des naissances
 d  Geburtenstatistik

3054 CUSTOMS STATISTICS
 f  Statistiques douanières
 d  Zollstatistik

3055 ECONOMIC STATISTICS
 f  Statistiques économiques
 d  Wirtschaftsstatistik

3056 EXPORT STATISTICS
 f  Statistiques d'exportations
 d  Exportstatistik

3057 FINANCIAL STATISTICS
 f  Statistiques financières
 d  Finanzstatistik

3058 FOREIGN TRADE
 STATISTICS
 f  Statistiques du commerce
 d  Aussenhandelsstatistik

3059 IMPORT STATISTICS
 f  Import statistiques
 d  Importstatistik

3060 INDUSTRIAL STATISTICS
 f  Statistiques industrielles
 d  Industriestatistik

3061 LABOUR FORCE STATISTICS;
 MANPOWER STATISTICS
 f  Statistiques de travail;
   Statistiques de main-
   d'oeuvre
 d  Arbeitskraftstatistik

3062 MICRO-ECONOMIC
 OPERATIONAL STATISTICS
 f  Statistiques micro-écono-
   miques
 d  Betriebsstatistik

3063 MIGRATION STATISTICS
 f  Statistiques migratoires;
   Statistiques de migration
 d  Wanderungsstatistik

3064 MONETARY STATISTICS
 f  Statistiques monétaires
 d  Monetäre Statistik

3065 OPTIMUM STATISTICS
 f  Estimateur optimum
 d  Beste statistische
   Masszahl

3066 PRODUCTION STATISTICS
 f  Statistiques de production
 d  Produktionsstatistik

3067 PUBLIC HEALTH
 STATISTICS
 f  Statistiques sanitaires
 d  Statistik des öffentlichen
   Gesundheitswesens

3068   SALES STATISTICS
       f   Statistiques des chiffres
           d'affaires
       d   Umsatzstatistik

3069   SCHOOL STATISTICS
       f   Statistiques scolaires
       d   Schulstatistik

3070   SOCIAL STATISTICS
       f   Statistiques sociales
       d   Sozialstatistik

3071   TRADE STATISTICS
       f   Statistiques commerciales
       d   Handelsstatistik

3072   STATISTICIAN
       f   Statisticien
       d   Statistiker

3073   STATISTICS BUREAU
       f   Service statistique
       d   Statistischer Dienst

3074   HOMELAND STUDY
       f   Monographie régionale
       d   Regionale Monographie

3075   OVERALL STUDIES
       f   Etudes d'ensemble
       d   Gesamtstudien

3076   SECTORIAL STUDY
       f   Etude sectorielle
       d   Sektorenanalyse

3077   SATURATION;
       DEGREE OF SATURATION
       f   Degré de saturation
       d   Sättigungsgrad

3078   OVERALL SUMMARY
       f   Synthèse globale
       d   Globalsynthese

3079   SURVEY SERVICES
       f   Services de recherches
       d   Untersuchungsdienst;
           Erhebungsdienst

3080   BRANCH AND SECTOR
       SURVEY
       f   Enquête par branches et
           par secteurs
       d   Branchen- und Sektoren-
           untersuchung

3081   CONTINUING SURVEYS
       f   Enquêtes permanentes
       d   Permanente Erhebungen

3082   ECONOMIC SURVEY
       f   Enquête économique;
           Etude économique;
           Aperçu économique
       d   Wirtschaftserhebung;
           Wirtschaftsübersicht

3083   HYDROGEOLOGICAL
       SURVEY
       f   Etude hydrogéologique
       d   Hydrologische Erhebung

3084   MANPOWER SURVEY
       f   Enquête sur la main-
           d'oeuvre
       d   Arbeitskräfteerhebung

3085   MAIL SURVEY
       f   Enquête par correspon-
           dance;
           Enquête postale
       d   Postbefragung

3086   MULTI-PURPOSE SURVEY
       f   Enquête à objectifs
           multiples
       d   Mehrzweckerhebung

3087   PILOT SURVEY;
       SAMPLE SURVEY
       f   Enquête pilote;
           Enquête expérimentale
       d   Versuchserhebung

3088   PRELIMINARY SURVEY
       f   Enquête préliminaire
       d   Vorerhebung

3089   SAVINGS SURVEY
       f   Enquête sur l'épargne
       d   Erhebung über Ersparnisse

3090 SOCIAL SURVEY
    f  Enquête sociale
    d  Sozialerhebung

3091 TABLE OF TABLES
    f  Liste des graphiques
    d  Liste der statistischen
       Tabellen

3092 COMPARATIVE TABLE
    f  Tableau comparatif
    d  Komparative Tabelle

3093 TECHNIQUES IN FIELD
    WORK
    f  Techniques d'enquêtes
    d  Techniken der Feldarbeit

3094 PRETEST
    f  Essai préliminaire
    d  Vortest

3095 THEORY OF DECISIONS
    f  Théorie des décisions
    d  Entscheidungstheorie

3096 TIME LAG
    f  Décalage
    d  Zeitlapsus

3097 TIME-SERIES
    f  Séries chronologiques
    d  Zeitreihen

3098 TOLERANCE LIMITS
    f  Limites d'acceptation
    d  Toleranzgrenzen

3099 TREND
    f  Evolution
    d  Entwicklungstendenz

3100 CURVILINEAR TREND;
    NON-LINEAR TREND
    f  Tendance curviligne;
       Tendance non-linéaire
    d  Nicht-linearer Trend

3101 ECONOMIC TREND
    f  Tendances économiques
    d  Ökonomischer Trend

3102 LINEAR TREND
    f  Tendance linéaire;
       Trend linéaire
    d  Linearer Trend

3103 SECULAR TREND;
    LONG-RUN TREND
    f  Tendance séculaire;
       Tendance à long terme
    d  Langfristiger Trend;
       Langfristige Tendenz

3104 TRIAL AND ERROR
    f  Système par itération
    d  Iterationssystem

3105 TURN-PIKE THEOREM;
    SAMUELSON
    f  "Turn-Pike" théorème
    d  "Turn-Pike" Theorem

3106 GIVEN UNIT
    f  Ensemble donné
    d  Gegebene Einheit

3107 VARIABLE
    f  Variable
    d  Variable

3108 VARIANCE
    f  Variance
    d  Varianz

3109 VERIFICATION;
    REVIEW;
    CHECKING
    f  Vérification
    d  Überprüfung

3110 WEIGHT
    f  Coefficient de pondération
    d  Gewichtung

3111 WORKING OUT OF
    STATISTICAL DOCUMENTA-
    TION
    f  Elaboration de la
       documentation statistique
    d  Ausarbeitung von statis-
       tischem Material

3112    YIELD PER UNIT
       f    Rendement par unité
       d    Ertrag je Einheit

# ENGLISH

Ability to invest 1513
Aboriginal groups 2733
Absenteeism 2327
Absolute deviation 2926
Absolute error 2937
Absorption capacity 1351
Academic authorities 2086
Accelerated development 114
Accelerated industrialization 973
Accelerated training 2291
Access road 1244
Accomodation road 1244
Accounting framework 2874
Accounting price 1575
Acculturation 2611
Achievement motivation 2612
Acquisition of skills 2087
Action programme 466
Adaptation plan 380
Additional instruction 2198
Adjustment of tariffs 2034
Adjustment process 2614
Administrative machinery 260
Administrative organization 261
Administrative problems 442
Administrative provisions 262
Administrative services 263
Adult literacy 2207
Ad valorem duty 1670
Advanced country 66
Advanced training 2290
Adviser 2088
Advisory aid 2089
African context 2644
African culture 2650
African elite 173
African industry 976
Africanism 18
Africanist 20
Africanization 21, 2615
African particularism 2616
African population 2617
African socialism 240
African society 2618
Africa south of the Sahara 4
After sale service 2019
Age and sex composition 2347
Age composition 2328
Age of dependency 2329
Age of industry 932
Age pyramid 2330

Age structure 2331
Aggregate 2876
Aggregate imports 1920
Aggregate output 372
Agrarian legislation 531
Agrarian reform 532
Agrarian socialism 241
Agreement for compensation 1782
Agreement on cooperation 1783
Agreement on economic
  cooperation 291
Agreement on tariffs 2035
Agreement on trade 1784
Agreement scheme 1781
Agricultural accounting 533
Agricultural advisory scheme 534
Agricultural bank 1615
Agricultural college 2097
Agricultural cooperatives 535
Agricultural credit 536, 1416
Agricultural development 537
Agricultural economics 538
Agricultural education 2113
Agricultural education
  specialist 2114
Agricultural engineer 539
Agricultural engineering 540
Agricultural equipment 633
Agricultural extension centre 541
Agricultural law 542
Agricultural machinery 543
Agricultural market 544
Agricultural planning 545
Agricultural policy 546
Agricultural processing
  industry 547
Agricultural produce 548
Agricultural production 549
Agricultural products 550
Agricultural programming 3003
Agricultural protectionism 551
Agricultural sector 553
Agricultural semi-nomadism 2778
Agricultural services 554
Agricultural statistics 3050
Agricultural taxation 1770
Agricultural training centre 2280
Agricultural unit 555
Agronomic research 552
Agronomization 558
Aid agencies 22

Self-determination 232
Self-development 120
Self-financing 1471
Self-help 233
Self-help housing 2725
Self-help institutions 234
Self-management 743
Self-sufficiency 236
Self-supply 2809
Self-sustained growth 339
Selling price 1993
Semi-arid country 2810
Semi-automatic machines 1037
Semi-finished product 1102
Semi-private bank 1629
Senior civil servants 510
Senior staff 2252
Service craft 891
Servicing facilities 1262
Sesame 791
Settlement 2811
Settlement of nomads 2813
Settlement pattern 2812
Shadow price 1581
Shadow rate 1713
Sheep breeding 795
Shelled groundnut 694
Shifting culture 2654
Shifting of the tax 1764
Shipping 1263
Shipping papers 1264
Shoe factory 1103
Shortage of capital 1386
Shortage of food 2385
Shortage of handicraft 2446
Shortage of modern equipment 1265
Shortage of senior personnel 2247
Shortage of specialized manpower
    2453
Shortage of staff 2528
Shortage of teachers 2246
Shortage of technical personnel 2248
Shortfall in skills 2249
Side effects 313
Sight debt 1440
Significant difference 3032
Silviculture hostility 796
Simulation theory 3033
Single-crop farming 640
Sinking fund 1486
Sisal 797

Sisal growing 691
Situation analysis 2881
Size of population 2510
Size of the enterprise 1104
Skilled labour 2423
Slaughterhouses 798
Slow growth 340
Slum clearance 2530
Slums 2815
Small crafts 892
Small farm 631
Small holding 631
Smallness of the national market
    2021
Small-scale industry 1021
Smuggling 2022
Social aid 2531
Social anthropology 2622
Social aspects 2532
Social assistance 2531
Social capital 1379
Social change 2816
Social classes 2533
Social control 2818
Social cost 1402
Social crisis 2819
Social desintegration 2820
Social development 121
Social disorganization 2821
Social environment 2534, 2690
Social inequality 2822
Social institutions 196
Social insurance 2535
Social integration 2823
Social investment project 1512
Social investments 1511
Socialist economy 170, 309
Social justice 2536
Social legislation 2429
Social mechanism 2824
Social mobility 2537
Social obligations 2825
Social Overhead Capital (S.O.C.)
    239
Social personality 2826
Social policy 2538
Social position 2539
Social progress 225
Social promoter 2540
Social relief 2531
Social responsibility 2827

Tone of the market 1940
Ton-kilometer 1275
Tonnage 2041
Tools 1115
Topography 1277
Top personnel 2223
Total credit 1427
Total exports and imports 1893
Tourism for pleasure 1116
Tourist centre 1120
Tourist industry 1121
Tourist lines 1122
Tourist traffic 1125
Town dwellers 2552
Town planning 435
Tractor 822
Trade agreement 1792
Trade and distribution 2051
Trade barriers 2042
"Trade creation" 2043
Trade deficit 2044
Trade exhibition 2045
Trade fair 2045
Trade markets 2046
Trade missions 2047
Trade pattern 2068
Trade promotion and marketing
    2048
Trade relations 2049
Trade statistics 3071
Trade trends 2050
Trade unions 2414
Trading agreement 1792
Trading partner 2077
Trading period 2076
Traditional commodity 2633
Traditional culture methods 2671
Traditional economy 2852
Traditional environment 2691
Traditional exchange 2699
Traditional exports 1894
Traditional fishing 661
Traditional form of security 2808
Traditional native authorities
    2773
Traditional society 2832
Traditional sources of energy
    (sun and wind) 913
Traditional structure 521
Traffic agreement 1278
Traffic needs 1279

Traffic requirements 1279
Traffic volume 1280
Trailer 1296
Trainee 2272
Training abroad 2302
Training activities 2274
Training assistance 2275
Training centre 2276
Training centre for cattle-rearing
    575
Training coordination 2277
Training course 2278
Training facilities 2279
Training farm 2280
Training machinery 2281
Training method 2282
Training of cadres 2310
Training officer 2283
Training of future staff 2311
Training of technicians 2312
Training of young people 2311
Training policy 2284
Training priorities 2285
Training programme 2286
Training promotion 2287
Training requirements 2288
Training strategy 2289
Trans-Cameroon railway 1224
Transcontinental movement 1206
Transfer of functions 527
Transfer of knowledge 2313
Transfer operations 1605
Transfer payments 1606
Transformation industry 1023
Transit agreement 1793
Transitional period 2078
Transit trade 2063
Transit traffic 1293
Transmigration 2553
Transportation accounting 1305
Transportation agency 1170
Transportation by air 1330
Trnasportation by helicopter 1326
Transportation charges 1306
Transportation company 1307
Transportation coordination 1308
Transportation cost 1163
Transportation economy 1309
Transportation equipment 1310
Transportation expert 1312
Transportation facilities 1311

# FRENCH

FRENCH

Période de remboursement 1590
Période de stagnation 512
Période de stockage 1270
Période de traite 2076
Période d'exécution 369
Période d'installation 348
Période donnée 2992, 2993
Période du rapport 2992
Période prae-européenne 2786
Période transitoire 2078
Personnalité sociale 2826
Personnel de formation à
   l'étranger 2225
Personnel d'hygiène publique 2221
Personnel étranger 2220
Personnel expatrié 2220
Personnel national 2481
Personnel scientifique 2222
Personnel supérieur 2252
Personnes en transit 1297
Perspectives commerciales 1818
Perspectives de développement 113,
   126
Perspectives démographiques 2508
Perspectives d'exportation 1881
Perspectives du commerce mondial
   2003
Perspectives économiques 145
Perte de devises 1665
Pertes au coûts 1443
Pertes économiques 360
Pertes en capital 1366
Petite construction individuelle
   2725
Petite exploitation 631
Petite industrie 1021
Pétrole brut 1075
Pétrole et dérivés 1069
Peuplement 2811
Phénomène de masse 2973
Philosophie de l'économie 147
Phytosociologie 760
Piassava 756
Pièce détachée 1105
Pilier de l'économie 311
Pipe-line 1076
Pisciculture 652
Pissave 756
Piste 1249, 1261
Pistes aériennes 1168
Plan d'action 379

Plan d'adaptation 380
Plan d'assainissement 386
Plan de stabilisation 388
Plan d'industrialisation 970
Plan d'investissements 1494
Plan économique 381
Plan global 382
Planificateur 392
Planificateur de l'éducation 2156
Planification agricole 545
Planification à long terme 429
Planification appliquée 417
Planification centralisée 418
Planification coloniale 419
Planification de la construction
   routière 1236
Planification de l'aide au
   développement 398
Planification de la main-d'oeuvre
   2440
Planification de la scolarisation
   2229
Planification de l'économie
   forestière 683
Planification de l'éducation 2157
Planification de l'enseignement
   2157
Planification de l'espace 433
Planification de l'investissement
   1495
Planification des eaux 436
Planification des grandes routes
   1189
Planification des ressources
   humaines 2387
Planification des revenus 426
Planification des salaires 2576
Planification du développement 421
Planification du transport 1317
Planification dynamique 422
Planification économique 423
Planification familiale 2378
Planification financière 1681
Planification fonctionnelle 431
Planification globale 432
Planification impérative 425
Planification indicative 427
Planification industrielle 952
Planification intégrale 420
Planification interrégionale 428
Planification nationale 430

Production mondiale 2084
Production planifiée 458
Production propre 452
Productions nouvelles 460
Production végétale 833
Production vivrière 674
Productivité 462
Productivité à l'hectare 2990
Productivité du travail 2409
Productivité sociale marginale
  202, 463
Produit 1820
Produit de base 223
Produit de substitution 1999
Produit des ventes 2016
Produit fini 923
Produit industriel 956
Produit local 443
Produit national 207
Produit principal 776, 1998
Produits agricoles 548
Produits agricoles de base 774
Produits chimiques 873
Produits d'algues 775
Produits de grande série 1046
Produits de la brousse 593
Produits d'exportation 1880
Produit secondaire 1101
Produit semi-fini 1102
Produits forestiers 2716
Produits palmiers 749
Produit transformé 1087
Produit tropical 2000
Professions rurales 2473
Programmation 3001
Programmation agraire 3003
Programmation industrielle 3004
Programmation linéaire 3005
Programme à moyen terme 468
Programme d'action 466
Programme de base 266
Programme de développement 98
Programme de formation 2286
Programme de l'enseignement 2103
Programme d'enseignement 2158
Programme de participation 469
Programme de promotion 23
Programme de travail 2594
Programme d'investissements 1498
Programme élargi 467
Programmes d'apprentissage 2090

Programmes de coopération 284
Progrès de moyens d'enseignement
  2189
Progrès économique 224
Progrès social 225
Progrès technique 226
Projection de la demande 483
Projection démographique 2493
Projection économique 484
Projet clef 475
Projet "clef en mains" 480
Projet d'accord 1781
Projet de budget 1640
Projet de construction 473
Projet d'investissement social
  1512
Projet du développement 99
Projet intégré 474
Projet non-rentable 481
Projet pilote 477
Projets de plan 378
Projets de planification 408
Projets d'industrialisation 972
Projets d'irrigation 703
Projets pour l'industrie 1016
Promotion de la formation 2287
Promotion de l'artisanat 894
Promotion du développement 108
Promotion industrielle 958
Propension à épargner 1587
Propension à inflation 1558
Propension marginale à
  consommer 485
Propriété foncière 713
Propriété industrielle 959
Propriétés d'Etat 809
Prospection pétrolière 1066
Protection de l'enfance 2587
Protection des cultures 590
Protection des investissements
  extérieures 1516
Protection douanière 1842
Protection du travail 2595
Protectionnisme 2004
Protectionnisme agricole 551
Protection sociale 2588
Protocoles multilatéraux 2005
Prototype 3006
Psychologie industrielle 960
Psychologie pédagogique 2159
Psychotechnique 960

# GERMAN